INTO

the

WESTERN

WINDS

Pioneer Boys Traveling the Overland Trails

Mary Barmeyer O'Brien

INTO

the

WESTERN

WINDS

Pioneer Boys Traveling the Overland Trails

TWODOT®

GUILFORD, CONNECTICUT
HELENA, MONTANA

AN IMPRINT OF THE GLOBE PEQUOT PRESS

A · TWODOT® · BOOK

Copyright © 2003 Mary Barmeyer O'Brien

TwoDot is a registered trademark of The Globe Pequot Press.

Map by Tony Moore; © The Globe Pequot Press

Library of Congress Cataloging-in-Publication Data
O'Brien, Mary Barmeyer.
Into the western winds: pioneer boys traveling the overland trails / Mary Barmeyer O'Brien.—1st ed.
        p. cm.
    Includes bibliographical references (p.) and index.
    ISBN 0-7627-1020-9
        1. Pioneer Children—West (U.S.)—Biography. 2. Pioneers —West (U.S.)—Biography. 3. Boys—West (U.S.)—Biography. 4. West (U.S.)—Biography. 5. Overland journeys to the Pacific—Anecdotes. 6. Frontier and pioneer life—West (U.S.)—Anecdotes. 7. West (U.S.)—Description and travel—Anecdotes. 8. West (U.S.)—History—1848-1860—Anecdotes. I. Title.

F593 .O275 2003
978'.02'08341—dc21   2002033905

Manufactured in the United States of America
First Edition/First Printing

This book is dedicated to the memory of my father,
Dr. George Henry Barmeyer.

CONTENTS

Acknowledgments xi

Introduction... xiii

A Raven Overhead:
The Story of Jesse A. Applegate 1

Wintering Alone in the Mountains:
The Story of Moses Schallenberger 13

Woodpecker Soup for Supper:
The Story of Henry and John Ferguson 23

Provisions to the Rescue:
The Story of Octavius M. Pringle 31

Above and Beyond the Call of Duty:
The Story of Welborn Beeson 41

If I Should Die Before I Wake:
The Story of Elisha Brooks 51

Barefoot Toward Zion:
The Story of Brigham H. Roberts 61

To the Land of Golden Shores:
The Story of Charles Frederick True 73

Trouble in Death Valley:
The Story of John Wells Brier 85

Bibliography 95

Index... 101

About the Author... 107

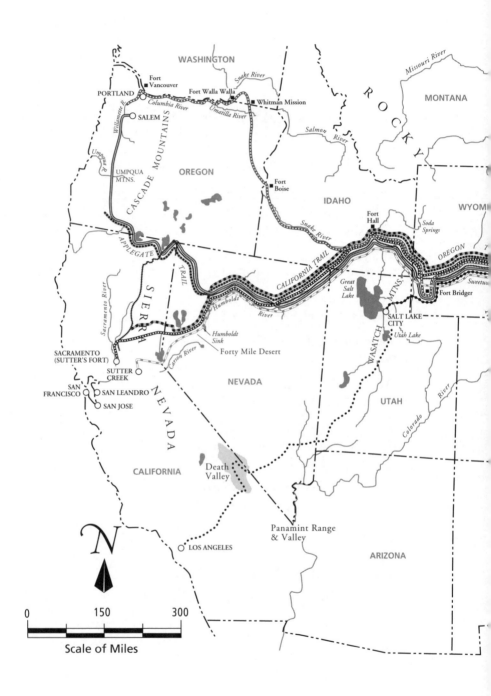

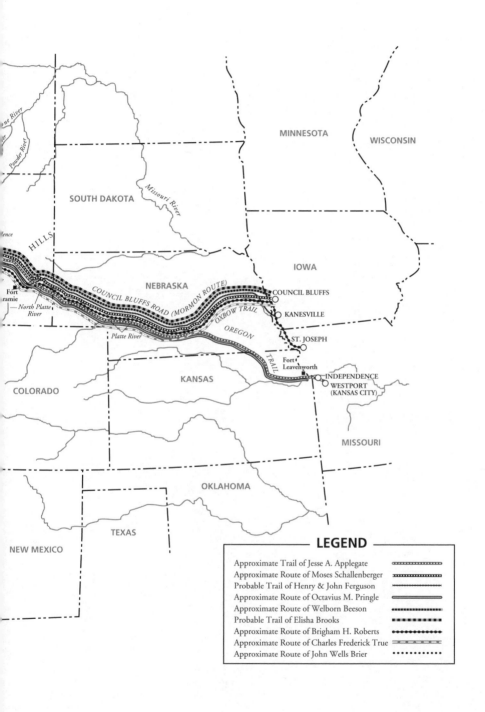

MINNESOTA

WISCONSIN

SOUTH DAKOTA

Missouri River

IOWA

Fort
aramie

— *North Platte River*

COUNCIL BLUFFS ROAD (MORMON ROUTE)

NEBRASKA

COUNCIL BLUFFS

KANESVILLE

OXBOW TRAIL

OREGON

Platte River

ST. JOSEPH

Fort
Leavenworth

TRAIL

KANSAS

INDEPENDENCE
WESTPORT
(KANSAS CITY)

COLORADO

MISSOURI

OKLAHOMA

NEW MEXICO

TEXAS

LEGEND

Approximate Trail of Jesse A. Applegate
Approximate Route of Moses Schallenberger
Probable Trail of Henry & John Ferguson
Approximate Route of Octavius M. Pringle
Approximate Route of Welborn Beeson
Probable Trail of Elisha Brooks
Approximate Route of Brigham H. Roberts
Approximate Route of Charles Frederick True
Approximate Route of John Wells Brier

ACKNOWLEDGMENTS

I would like to express my heartfelt appreciation and thanks to those who helped see *Into the Western Winds* to completion, including:

- The ten courageous, stalwart boys whose stories are told within these pages, for recording the details of their wagon journeys, for sharing their personalities and experiences across the centuries, and for leaving behind their remarkable legacies.

- Charlene Patterson and Shelley Wolf, my editors at The Globe Pequot Press, for their ongoing support and fine work.

- Friend and fellow writer Maggie Plummer, for willingly critiquing each chapter, for offering her insights and helpful suggestions, and for generally keeping me "rolling along" with her humor and positive interest.

- The staff at Polson City Library, for help in carrying out my research, especially Marilyn Trosper, whose interest and expertise encouraged and assisted me, as always. I am also very grateful to Allison Reed and Rita Bell for their unfailing patience in locating and ordering interlibrary loan materials for me.

- My family and friends, one and all, for their interest, love, and encouragement.

- Susan Snyder of the University of California's Bancroft Library, for assistance in obtaining the memoir of Henry and John Ferguson.

- Carol Harbison-Samuelson, library manager and photo archivist for the Southern Oregon Historical Society, for her great help in providing material about the life of Welborn Beeson.

- Edward B. Jorgenson, volunteer for the Southern Oregon Historical Society, for his insights into the personality and character of Welborn Beeson.
- Bill Slaughter, archivist for the Family and Church History Department of the Church of Jesus Christ of Latter-day Saints, for help in locating photographs of Brigham H. Roberts.
- Craig A. Smith, information specialist for the Oregon State Library in Salem, and Joan Marie Meyering, for their assistance in obtaining the photograph of Octavius Pringle.
- Rebecca Shotwell of the Sierra Club, for her help in locating the article "Trailing the Forty-niners Through Death Valley," by Carl I. Wheat, from the June 1939 *Sierra Club Bulletin*.
- Caitlin Lewis, assistant librarian at San Francisco's William E. Colby Memorial Library, for her assistance in obtaining the article "Robinson Crusoe in the Sierra Nevada: The Story of Moses Schallenberger at Donner Lake in 1844–45," from the May 1951 *Sierra Club Bulletin*.
- Ellen Harding of the California State Library (California History Section) and Chris Brewer of Bear State Library's Vintage Resources, for their help in locating the photographs of John Wells Brier and his family.
- Susan Seyl, director of Image Collections for the Oregon Historical Society's Photography Department, for her work in locating a photograph of Jesse A. Applegate.

Special Note: The diaries, oral histories, reminiscences, and memoirs recorded or written by the boys in this volume (as children or later as adults) are cited in the bibliography at the end of this book. I occasionally have used their own words to help tell their stories. All excerpts are presented as closely to the original as possible, including unusual spelling, punctuation, and grammar.

INTRODUCTION

Going west.

Those were magical words to boys of the mid-1800s, who imagined leaving behind the drudgery and chores that characterized their young lives and setting off on a glorious all-summer camping trip. There would be no baths or schoolbooks, no plowing or harvesting. Instead their families would travel the legendary overland trails to Oregon, California, or other destinations. They would cross clear, blue rivers and scale the far-off Rockies—an amazing thought to boys who, having spent their lives in flat Midwestern villages, had never even laid eyes on a mountain. Huge herds of bison would roam nearby. In the cool summer evenings, families would gather around crackling campfires while friends strummed guitars and mothers cooked savory antelope steaks and flaky biscuits. Along the way they would trade their trinkets with the native peoples of the West and stop at the forts they had read about in guidebooks. All the while they would travel steadily and surely toward the West, where according to word of mouth, gold nuggets waited to be plucked from tumbling streams and farmland was so rich that abundant crops sprang forth without the usual backbreaking work.

At the beginning of their journeys, pioneer boys did indeed romp behind the wagons, holding foot races and splashing each other in cool creeks. But almost immediately play gave way to hardship, and before long these same boys were guarding the wagons with loaded rifles and trudging hot, monotonous miles with sore feet and little sustenance. They soon discovered that even the best-planned journeys could go terribly wrong, and that their own never-ending hard work was vital to their families' very survival.

Before long, most had experienced the reality of the overland trails. Pelting rain or snow chilled them to the bone, high winds blew their tents down, and mud stalled their progress. Wagons broke. Food ran out, and water—a simple cold drink of water—was not to be found along the many stretches of hot, dry desert. Fleas infested their bedding, and mosquitoes arose in clouds along the trails. There were violent encounters with the Sioux, Pawnee, and other native tribes, who were deeply disturbed at the vast migration of people invading their lands. Oxen, which were not only work animals but also beloved companions with names like Pete, Whitey, and Old Blue, died of exhaustion. Mountain fever attacked the healthiest of wagon travelers, and cholera raged along the trails, claiming the lives of loved ones.

A few wrote diaries as they trekked westward. Others later wrote memoirs about their remarkable journeys or sent letters to loved ones describing their trips. Seventeen-year-old Welborn Beeson kept a careful, detailed diary as he traveled to Oregon's Rogue River Valley with his parents (and for many years afterward), recording events even when he was sick. Later in his life, he wrote that his diary "will never be read by anyone, and it makes me feel sad." Little did he imagine that his outstanding journal would become a treasured document studied by many for its authentic and precise look at pioneer life.

Occasionally boys mentioned a hearty meal, a campfire sing-along, or a nap in the warm sun. More often the harried emigrant youngsters wrote about fording rivers raging with spring runoff, huddling in their wagons during violent lightning storms, searching time and again for strayed or stolen cattle, and helping with wagon repairs. These boys, who became young men overnight, told of eating bizarre foods in desperate hunger: woodpecker stew, for example, or shreds of stringy coyote meat. One even remembers a fellow traveler gnawing a tallow candle for sustenance.

Of necessity, boys were given chores that demanded adult responsibility and dependability. One of the most important was herding spare livestock behind the wagon trains, a difficult job in choking dust, but one that was vital to a successful journey. Extra oxen and horses meant the difference between being stranded in dangerous territory and safely reaching the destination. In the rear, away from their parents' watchful eyes, pioneer boys found enough mischief (snowballs to throw, stories to swap, tricks to play) to lighten the monotony and stress of the journey.

Some were needed to drive the wagons and watch over the corralled trains at night. Sixteen-year-old Charles Frederick True wrote of the times he and a companion stood guard. Another teenager, Moses Schallenberger, and young brothers John and Henry Ferguson actually stayed behind to protect wagons when their parties had to abandon the cumbersome loads and hurry on to civilization.

Each of the boys selected for this collection found the resourcefulness to rise to the unusual circumstances of his overland journey. Whether traveling alone in the wilderness like fourteen-year-old Octavius Pringle, trudging across Death Valley like six-year-old John Wells Brier, or boating the rapids on the Columbia River like young Jesse Applegate, each summoned the courage to help his family complete a remarkable trip west. Their stories are their legacies, thoughtfully put down on paper in later years, or scrawled in boyish haste in diaries as the trek unfolded.

A RAVEN OVERHEAD

The Story of Jesse A. Applegate

Young Jesse A. Applegate stared at the rushing sweep of water that carried his family's skiff downstream. The powerful current of the Columbia River pulled the small boat toward the whirling rapids ahead. At the oars Jesse's father and uncle were nearly powerless against the water's force. Jesse could see the white faces of his brothers and cousin in another skiff a short way off, and while he watched, their boat veered off the course set by the party's guide, bucking violently in the roiling waves. Maybe his Aunt Cynthia's superstitious remark at a recent overnight camping place would prove to be true after all. "There is going to be a death in the family," she had predicted. "See that raven flying over the camp?"

At first seven-year-old Jesse was alarmed by his aunt's words. But even as a young child, Jesse knew that his family was strong and capable. For the past few months, they had met every challenge the primitive overland trail had presented with energy and success. Home was now hundreds of miles behind them on the banks of the Osage River in Missouri, where Jesse and his brothers and cousins had spent their early childhoods picking sweet wild plums in the

1

tangled undergrowth and slipping into the cool water when their mothers weren't watching.

The Applegate men started talking about going to Oregon long before they actually began the covered wagon journey with their families in the spring of 1843. Lindsay Applegate, Jesse's father, joined two of his brothers, Charles and Jesse, and nearly one thousand other emigrants for the trip west. They planned to drive a huge herd of cattle with them, an undertaking the elder Jesse Applegate described in his later work, *A Day with the Cow Column*. The younger Jesse also recorded his memories of the trip later in life, putting down the impressions of the journey from a seven-year-old's perspective, which he called *Recollections of My Boyhood*.

Near Independence, Missouri, the wagons and cattle assembled. Somewhere amid the noise and commotion were Lindsay Applegate's three wagons, one of which was loaded with provisions, and his many cattle. The Applegate brothers knew the trip would be grueling. At that early date, only a few missionaries had undertaken the overland trek, and covered wagons were new to the trail. But a thousand emigrants—whose venture was known in history as the Great Emigration or the Great Migration of 1843—created an unprecedented and formidable protection against the rigors of the journey. The Applegates themselves were young, energetic, and intelligent. Their adventurous spirits combined with sheer determination and strength made them good candidates for this first experimental wagon trip. With them would travel the well-respected and experienced Dr. Marcus Whitman, the famous missionary who had already established his mission near Walla Walla and was returning there from a journey east. Also along on the trip was an elderly man whom Jesse fondly called "Uncle Mack," but whose real name was Alexander McClellan. A family friend, he had stayed with the

Applegates back home in Missouri and was making the trip west with them.

The group started out. Crossing the swollen Kansas River was a six-day project, but after that the group pressed ahead, roughly following the Little Blue River until they reached the Platte River near Grand Island. There were about 120 wagons and hundreds upon hundreds of loose cattle and horses. This caused dissent, according to Jesse's uncle, since some families had only their own teams while others brought large herds of animals. The two groups soon split so the families with less livestock could travel without the encumbrance of "the cow column." Jesse and his family stayed with the animal train, which was led by his uncle, the elder Jesse Applegate. The cow column traveled so efficiently that they were able to keep up with the less encumbered train, and the two groups stayed more or less together throughout Plains Indian territory. All his life, Jesse would remember the undulating masses of animals, their pungent odors, and the way they trampled the vegetation, first into the mud and later into the dust as the summer progressed.

Although Jesse's memories of the westward journey were somewhat jumbled in their geographic accuracy, his recollections were vivid when it came to events of boyish interest. Like other children, he was fascinated by the party's Indian encounters. He admired the Caw men for their tall, proud stature and wrote that he wasn't afraid, even when he saw a war party "armed with bows, spears, war-clubs, tomahawks, and knives." He also recalled the famous landmarks they passed and notable incidents that etched themselves on his memory, including a violent midnight rainstorm with crashing thunder, blinding lightning, and cold water pouring into his sleeping tent—and Uncle Mack, who picked him up and kindly put him in one of the wagons.

The diaries of fellow travelers state that the foul weather was more than just a storm, but instead was day after day of wet, cold weather. They pushed on through deep mud and slept fitfully in soaked bedding. Streams turned into rushing torrents. But by the fifth week, when Jesse's wagon train reached the Platte River and turned west along its south bank, the weather had turned warm. Uncle Jesse marveled at the scenic beauty, writing: "To those who have not been on the Platte my powers of description are wholly inadequate to convey an idea of the vast extent and grandeur of the picture, and the rare beauty and distinctness of its detail."

Everyone was tired after the previous weeks of wet, uncomfortable nights. Teamsters dozed in the warm sunshine as the wagons progressed up the gentle, straight Platte River on a relatively easy trail intersected only by old, deep grooves worn by bison coming to drink at the water's edge. There were no trees along its banks and the water was wide, shallow, and so sandy that the women found deep sediment in the bottoms of their coffeepots. Some westward travelers, including Uncle Jesse, described the river as "too thick to drink and too thin to plow."

Young Jesse and his friends were assigned the chore of collecting dried buffalo chips for campfire fuel. While out on the grasslands, the boys loved to watch the huge numbers of prairie dogs. The appealing animals would pop up from their multitudes of holes to watch the travelers pass by and then disappear in a flash. Antelope and rabbits "were everywhere," Jesse reported. So were mosquitoes, which plagued the travelers along the river bottoms.

Crossing the South Platte with difficulty (another six-day undertaking that included July Fourth), the group pressed on toward the Sweetwater River in today's southern Wyoming. Young Jesse looked forward to their arrival there so he could taste the water he knew must be delicious and sugary. Finally reaching the riverbank, he ran down and took a big gulp of the clear water, but like many emigrant children, he was "greatly disappointed, for the water was very common indeed, and not sweet." Likewise he was later misled by the name of Green River, which was filled with water of a "white crystal clearness," not the deep green he had anticipated.

The emigrants stopped at Fort Laramie—a welcome bit of civilization—and then crossed the Continental Divide at South Pass, where they considered themselves officially in Oregon Territory. Despite having traveled hundreds of miles, they were only about halfway to their destination. Concerned that it was already mid-August, they hurried on to Fort Bridger in the far southwestern corner of today's state of Wyoming. Hoping to restock their supplies, the travelers were disappointed by the paltry stores and exorbitant prices they found at both forts. But the trail, by then steep and rough, entered an area with abundant game: elk, deer, wild goats, ducks, geese, and even trout, which they had never tasted before. Idaho's Soda Springs and geyserlike Steamboat Springs amazed Jesse, and he recalled these fascinating landmarks all his life. He also remembered meeting the famous explorer John Frémont and his companions there.

By the end of August, they had reached Fort Hall in today's state of Idaho. No wagons had ever traveled beyond this point, but the emigrants, encouraged by Marcus Whitman, were determined not to abandon theirs. From there on, new trail had to be broken. Jesse recalled that this was "very heavy work for the now somewhat jaded teams." The emigrants themselves were feeling the effects of the long summer on the trail. Just as their exhaustion began to set in, the most difficult part of the trail loomed ahead.

They camped on a high plateau above the Snake River, trading clothing for dried salmon with the Snake and Shoshone Indians and taking time to remove prickly pear spines from their bare feet. Sagebrush replaced grass, making it difficult to find forage for the animals. During part of this long, hot stretch, Jesse's family traveled alone to avoid dissent in the ranks, rejoining the group near Fort Boise. By that point the emigrants often broke into small groups for travel, loosely staying near the others and merging again for difficult areas of the trail.

Jesse's mother had warned him never to ride in the wagon carrying the family's provisions, but one day the temptation was too great. He climbed up beside the drowsy hired driver and tried to crack the whip over the oxen's heads. The effort caused him to slip off the wagon and fall to the ground between the oxen's hooves and the heavy front wheels of the wagon, which rolled over him. The hind wheels followed, despite Jesse's efforts to wriggle out of the way, and rolled over his legs. Although other emigrant children were badly hurt or even killed in similar accidents, Jesse was only slightly injured, and was more concerned about hiding the evidence of his disobedience from his mother. When she saw him having trouble standing and walking, she guessed the truth and, instead of scolding him as he feared, hugged him in utter relief over his narrow escape. He recovered without lasting effects.

The emigrants pushed on past Fort Boise, the Grande Ronde Valley, and the Blue Mountains in today's northeastern Oregon, where the going was extremely rough, and a road had to be hacked through the beautiful timber. Summer was gone, and snow greeted them. Jesse recalled his tired, cold march through the area and the contrasting pleasantness of the Umatilla River Valley with its abundant aspen and ripe berries. From there they veered north to the Whitman Mission, where Marcus and Narcissa Whitman had established their home among the Cayuse Indians. Because winter was near, they replenished their supplies but didn't linger, heading directly for Fort Walla Walla, a Hudson's Bay Company post on the Columbia River. There they halted to prepare for their journey down the river, deciding to temporarily abandon the wagons and livestock at Fort Walla Walla and make the remainder of the trip by boat. The large wagon party had splintered along the way, so by then only about ten families, including those of the three Applegate brothers, remained in the group. Jesse's father and uncles, along with elderly Uncle Mack and the other men, built small boats that would each carry eight to ten people down the Columbia to the Willamette River.

Jesse remembered vividly their first days on the river. He compared the gentle swaying and rocking of the skiff to riding on "a grape vine swing" and he reveled in the splashing, swirling water around them. For a few days the rough areas with strong wind frightened him, but he soon lost his apprehension and decided that the wild rocking and fast current in the rapids were great fun, especially since his capable father and uncles were at the oars. Camps were made on either side of the vast river, usually on a narrow strip of land between the water and the rocky bluffs along each shore. It was at one of these early river camps that Jesse's Aunt Cynthia made her unusual comment that seeing a raven flying overhead could mean an upcoming death in the family.

The river stretched on as the travelers faced the perpetual western wind that buffeted the small skiffs on white-capped waves. Dark basalt cliffs and steep hillsides rose from the water, and above were plateaus of golden grasses dotted with gray-green sage and etched with an occasional coulee. Mount Hood rose to a perfect white peak far downstream. Sometimes the group passed small islands fringed with low green bushes, and Jesse often saw Indians in "shapely" and "neatly finished" canoes that had been made from logs. One of these Indian men became their temporary guide, riding in the front of

Jesse's skiff. The emigrants learned from the local peoples what indigenous foods were edible and added acorns, roots, bulbs, and berries to their dwindling provisions.

On a day they would remember with lasting sadness, Jesse saw the rapids ahead but was not afraid, especially with their native guide in the bow of the boat. As the skiff picked up speed and began leaping from breaker to breaker, Jesse "began to think this was no ordinary rapid, but felt reassured when I noticed that the older people sat quietly in their places and betrayed no sign of fear." The babies had even fallen asleep with the rocking motion. His father and Uncle Jesse were at the oars when everyone noticed that the skiff holding Uncle Mack, two young men, and three boys— Jesse's brothers, Warren (about nine) and Elisha (about eleven), and their cousin Edward (also about nine)—was off course.

To their horror, they watched the skiff disappear into a deep whirlpool. The men and boys slipped into the icy, roaring water with shouts of alarm and were carried downstream. Rescue was impossible, although Lindsay and the older Jesse Applegate dropped their oars and prepared to jump into the raging river to save them. They were held back by their wives, who feared that everyone would be lost if the men left their posts. Jolted back to reality, the men quickly steered their craft around a huge jagged rock they had nearly been dashed upon, and brought their boat safely to shore.

Anguished, the survivors hunted for their children and friends. Fortunately, Elisha saved himself by swimming and diving under the most ferocious waves until he reached a rock island. One of the young men grabbed a feather bed tick as it floated by and used it to reach safety, and the other young man was saved as well. Uncle Mack caught young Edward Applegate and attempted to help him to shore, but his strength gave out. Unwilling to save himself at the expense of the boy, he held on until they both disappeared, never to be seen again.

Jesse's brother Warren drowned as well. Although the families searched the river and its banks, no trace was ever found of him. Heavy with grief, Jesse must have wondered what he would ever do without Warren's companionship and brotherhood. His mother and Aunt Cynthia wept openly over the terrible loss of their sons, and the men were heavyhearted as they faced the days ahead. There was no choice but to finish the trip without their loved ones, but the families wondered if, indeed, the trip had been worth its horrible price.

More danger lay ahead. The Dalles was a relatively narrow, swift, rocky point in the river, difficult and dangerous to navigate. The women and children walked this stretch while the men struggled through with the boats. Avoiding the black, rocky shoreline and its cliffs, the men fought the current to avoid colliding the skiffs and brought them safely through the rapids. The next obstacle was the Cascades, where the boats had to be portaged.

At Fort Vancouver, they met the famous and kindly Dr. John McLoughlin of the Hudson's Bay Company. Here the small group divided, and the Applegate families headed across the Columbia to the mouth of the Willamette River. Not certain where they wished to settle, the group traveled up the Willamette, finally deciding to leave the boats and cross overland to the place where the first Methodist mission in the Willamette Valley had been located a few years before. There they found three abandoned log cabins under one roof and settled in for their first warm, wet winter in Oregon. The children attended school, which in Jesse's memory was a "cold and cheerless place," while the adults struggled to make do without the bedding, furnishings, and cooking utensils that had been lost along with their loved ones in the Columbia River tragedy.

The following year, still grieving for their lost sons and good friend, the families moved to the Salt Creek Valley near today's town of Dallas, Oregon. There they sent for the wagons and live-stock left behind at Fort Walla Walla. All that was left of Jesse's father's three wagons were four rear wheels, which the family used to make two carts. After a few years, each Applegate family had established a new farm, and the children spent their days hunting, fishing, gathering wild berries and nuts in the woods and creating their own toys and entertainment. There were always chores to be done, as well. In 1846, in an effort to spare later Oregon emigrants the terrible experience of losing friends and family members to the Columbia River's wild waters, Jesse's father and uncle, along with several others, scouted and pioneered a new route to the Oregon valleys that avoided the mighty river entirely. This new route, later known as the Applegate Trail, circled around and entered Oregon from the south.

Life was pleasant, but the Salt Creek area was not destined to be the Applegates' final home. Seven years later, the three brothers again moved their families, this time to southern Oregon's fertile Umpqua River Valley. There Jesse lived the remainder of his child-hood. The Applegates became well-known all over Oregon, and several of them, including his father and uncles, rose to prominence in the budding territory.

Although Jesse's memoir ends at this point, historical records show that he received an excellent education as he grew into an adult and eventually became a teacher and then a school superintendent. He married Virginia Watson and the two had seven children. Eventually he chose law for his lifelong profession and practiced at both Dallas and Salem for many years.

Throughout his long life, Jesse A. Applegate never forgot his journey west. In later years, when he recorded his reminiscences, he

JESSE A. APPLEGATE LATER IN LIFE.
OREGON HISTORICAL SOCIETY, OrHi 44

made an effort to tell them exactly as his seven-year-old mind had seen them, full of wonder and glory and boyish mischief. As a part of the first group of emigrants to carve out the Oregon Trail, Jesse remembered the great undertaking with excitement and a sense of adventure, until the tragedy on the Columbia stole his loved ones—and his childish innocence.

But Jesse and his extended family had to put the past behind them and go on with their lives. In this they succeeded by becoming statesmen, scholars, wise parents, and leaders. Today the state of Oregon has countless landmarks and historical records dedicated to the name "Applegate," the strong and charismatic family of which young Jesse was a part. ▨

WINTERING ALONE IN THE MOUNTAINS

The Story of Moses Schallenberger

Moses Schallenberger watched in dismay from the doorway of his makeshift log cabin. It seemed as though the snow would never stop falling here in the high Sierra Nevada. He had dug his way out through the tall drifts that piled up against the exit, but his isolated shelter was nearly buried. Back home in the gentle hills of the Midwest, there had never been snowfall like this.

Seventeen-year-old Moses considered his lonely plight. It was December, and there was no getting out of these mountains now. Even if he could escape, the California settlements were on the far side of the rocky cliffs and granite ridges. Wild animals he had counted on for his winter's food supply were gone, driven by harsh conditions to lower elevations. The snow was so deep he couldn't even fish in the nearby lake. At least he had the six wagons that his fellow travelers, who had hurried on ahead, had abandoned until spring.

It was 1844 when Moses set out from Missouri with his sister and her husband, Dr. and Mrs. John Townsend, and other emigrants headed for both Oregon and California. They were part of the famous Stevens-Townsend-Murphy Party, a small, strong, cooperative group of men, women, and children who, later in the journey, scouted and opened the first wagon trail over the Sierra Nevada. Moses was appointed, along with Dr. Townsend, to keep a detailed log of the journey. The log was eventually lost, but Moses's memories of the trip were later recorded and preserved.

It was mid-May when the party began its journey from near Council Bluffs on the Missouri River. The group traveled up the Platte River, swimming its reluctant cattle across tributaries and encountering several tribes of Indians. Like most emigrants of the time, they were fearful of the native people they met. Each night they corralled their wagons and put the train under careful guard. Moses and his friend John Murphy were selected as corporals and spent their hours after dark making sure the guards were awake and alert.

The two young men also helped to provide the camp with fresh meat. Huge herds of bison roamed the Plains, not to mention the thousands of antelope and smaller animals that hid in the long grasses. Moses and John hunted with eagerness and were able to provide enough meat not only for the moment, but also for part of the long, unknown stretch ahead. On one embarrassing occasion they returned to camp empty-handed, having lost their guns and ammunition somewhere in the undulating waves of grass, but usually the hunters were successful in feeding their comrades.

The wagon train made good progress to Fort Laramie, where several days were spent trading with the nearby Sioux for ponies, horses, and moccasins. At Independence Rock they stopped and camped for a week to hunt and preserve meat before resuming the journey up the Sweetwater River and over the Continental Divide at South Pass. They then moved toward the Green River by a new cutoff route, a desolate stretch that saved them miles but caused them to suffer terribly from lack of water. The parched cattle broke away and bolted for the Big Sandy River, where Moses and his companions found them later near a Sioux war camp.

Pushing on toward Fort Hall, they came across an old mountain man named Thomas L. "Peg-leg" Smith, who traded his healthy ponies for some of the travelers' worn-out horses. When they reached the fort, they replenished their flour for a dollar a pound. There the trail forked, and the California-bound emigrants said good-bye to their fellow travelers heading to Oregon. Moses and his relatives turned south with the Stevens-Townsend-Murphy Party, which at that point numbered about eleven wagons and about fifty men, women, and children.

The group soon reached the Humboldt River in today's northern Nevada. The summer was fast waning, and there were still hundreds of miles to go. They pressed on, enduring the monotonous, hot trail along the Humboldt and relying upon the winding river for water. When, after many days of slow progress, they arrived at the famous "Sink," where the water flowed underground and desert stretched ahead, Moses's group stopped for a week to rest the animals and decide upon the route to take. There was no existing wagon trail over the Sierra Nevada in 1844, and the party prepared to search its own way across the desert and over the mountains ahead.

An elderly Indian man, whom the travelers called Truckee, guided the group's scouts across the perilous forty-mile-long desert to the river now known as the Truckee in present-day eastern Nevada, and he showed them where the river cut through the nearly impassable Sierra Nevada. The route was untested for wagon travel and very rough, but it was a viable passageway through the treacherous mountains. By then it was late autumn, and the emigrants were worried about being trapped by snow on the eastern slopes. Provisions were getting low, but there was plenty of game for food.

At first the trip up the river went well. There was abundant water and grass for the cattle and wood for campfires. The weather held. As they gained altitude, however, the terrain became rougher, and the travelers were forced to use the rocky streambed for a trail. They struggled on, battling fatigue, occasional light snowfalls, and problems with the oxen's hooves, which were painfully softened by plodding in the water. The men splashed beside them up the icy river, urging them on. As the hills closed in on the narrow waterway, the river twisted and turned through heavy undergrowth. Step by step, the party ascended. More snow fell.

At a fork in the river, the cold, weary travelers stopped and camped. Here they split up, with a small group on horseback traveling up the main stream, which turned southwest, and the others inching the wagons up the tributary that came from the west. Moses and Dr. Townsend were with the wagon party; Moses's sister went with the horseback group.

A short distance upstream the wagon travelers came to what was later named Donner Lake after the famous Donner Party, who would meet with starvation there two years later. At the lake several of the families decided that, given the exhausted condition of the oxen and the rugged terrain, they would leave their wagons behind until they could reach the California settlements and return with fresh stock animals. Among them was Dr. Townsend, who had brought along a load of valuable goods to sell in California. Moses and two companions volunteered to stay behind and guard the wagons.

A few of the others decided to try to take their wagons over the remaining mountains again, despite the discouraging prospects. By then the snow was reportedly two feet deep, but they pushed

THE LAKE WHERE MOSES SCHALLENBERGER SPENT THE WINTER,
LATER CALLED DONNER LAKE.
THE ANDREW J. RUSSELL COLLECTION, OAKLAND MUSEUM OF CALIFORNIA

toward the summit, unloading and carrying their loads up the inclines by hand. Then the tired teams were doubled and the empty wagons were pulled up. All went well until a ten-foot-high vertical rock wall stopped them. There didn't seem to be any way to get the wagons beyond that point, but, upon inspection, a small passage-way up the cliff was discovered. The oxen could climb it in single file without their yokes. Once at the top, their yokes were replaced and then chained to the wagons below. With the oxen pulling from the top of the cliff and the men pushing from the bottom, the wag-ons were lifted over the rock wall. After that it was a short distance to the headwaters of the Yuba River.

The group was the first party to bring wagons over the moun-tains into California. When a heavy snowfall halted them on the Yuba, the women and children set up camp while most of the able-bodied men set off on foot for the settlements. They expected to be able to return immediately with help and supplies. Little did they know that their families would be snowed in for most of the winter.

Back at the lake, Moses and his two older companions, Joseph Foster and Allen Montgomery, felt they were in little danger. They thought there was plenty of game, and they had two bony cattle, left behind because they were too worn-out to continue the jour-ney. Furthermore, the Midwesterners didn't imagine that the snow would get any deeper or that it would remain on the ground all winter. They built a rough, windowless log cabin that measured about twelve feet by fourteen feet and covered it with rawhide and brush. A rude chimney made of rocks and logs stood at one end. The door, according to Moses, was never shut; it let in the only daylight.

Dragging blankets and quilts from the wagons, the three made warm beds and built a fire. Unconcerned, they watched the fluffy snow continue to fall. The weather wasn't too cold, and they

18

assumed the snow would melt soon and they would be able to hunt. But a week passed. Temperatures dropped and the snow kept falling. Finally they killed the two cows, but the poor, thin creatures offered little meat—certainly not enough to feed two men and a growing teenager for long. It was only late November or early December, and Moses related that "we began to fear that we should all perish in the snow."

Discouraged, they realized the wild game, except perhaps for a few foxes and coyotes whose tracks they had seen, had been forced to the lower elevations. Soon half the beef was gone, and even collecting firewood was almost impossible. The drifts were by then ten feet deep. "Death, the fearful, agonizing death by starvation, literally stared us in the face," Moses recalled.

Taking the hickory bows from the wagons and strong rawhide to form webbing, they fashioned homemade snowshoes to the best of their knowledge. Fastening them to their feet front and back, the three at least were able to navigate the drifts for firewood. Their rough contraptions with their untraditional design, however, collected snow on top, so the wearers had to lift a heavy load with each step.

Still, the only choice seemed to be to start for the settlements on foot. Drying some of the remaining beef, they set out, each with two blankets and a rifle. Shortly after they began the long climb to the summit, Moses started experiencing terrible cramps. He spent the day in agony, falling down in pain and dragging his heavy snowshoes through the snow to keep up with his companions. The three spent the night together at the summit, struggling to stay warm and worrying about the outcome of their journey. In the morning it was clear that Moses could not finish the trip. There was only one choice: He must return to the cabin while the others went on. His companions reluctantly agreed, and they promised to return for him with help if they made it to the settlements. With a sad hand-shake that he felt would be their last, Moses returned to the snowed-in cabin. Later, he recounted his desolate feelings: "The feeling of loneliness that came over me as the two men turned away I cannot express, though it will never be forgotten, while the 'Good-by, Mose,' so sadly and reluctantly spoken, rings in my ears to-day."

Moses made his way back down the mountain, reaching the cabin so exhausted that he had to lift his feet over the doorsill with his hands. But a good night's sleep revived him, and the next day he discovered some traps that Captain Elisha Stevens had left behind in one of the wagons. Strapping on his crude snowshoes again, he noted the tracks of foxes or coyotes on top of the crusty snow. Setting the traps carefully, he waited.

By the next morning he had caught an emaciated coyote. Moses took the carcass back to the cabin and skinned and roasted it, but the meat was disgusting. He tried boiling it, but even that didn't help the revolting flavor and texture. Still, it was meat, and it lasted him three days. His next trapping expedition resulted in two foxes whose meat was so delicious to the nearly starving Moses that he had a hard time making it last. From then on, he ate mostly fox meat, but he was continually anxious about the supply of food run-ning out. Once he shot and cooked a crow that flew near the cabin and discovered the meat was nearly as bad as coyote. He had enough coffee to make one cup, which he saved for Christmas Day.

"My life was more miserable than I can describe," Moses said later. Night after night he lay awake in the darkness with utter silence engulfing him. He worried about what had become of the rest of his wagon party, especially his sister and brother-in-law, and about what he would do if the supply of foxes ran out. In the day-light hours, he continued to trap, saving the coyotes he caught as an emergency food source. The days and nights seemed to stretch on forever. Passing time became one of his biggest challenges. Stuck in the tiny cabin, he tried to sleep late to make the days go by faster. Fortunately, his brother-in-law had filled one part of a wagon with books, so day after day, Moses read them to pass the long hours. At night he lighted big fires and read by their flickering light. Many times he spoke the words aloud to "break the oppressive stillness." The months, Moses said, "seemed years."

Finally one evening in late February, Moses saw a man laboring toward the cabin on snowshoes. With heart pounding in excitement, he peered into the distance. Relief and thankfulness overcame him. It was Dennis Martin, one of the men from his wagon party who, Moses later discovered, had made it to the settlements for the winter. "My feelings can be better imagined than described," Moses said.

Martin immediately set Moses's fears about his fellow travelers to rest, assuring him that both his sister's horseback party and the men on foot had arrived safely in California. Even those still stranded with their wagons on the Yuba River were alive and safe. An adept outdoorsman, Martin had set out to take provisions to the snowed-in families and to help them to the lower elevations. Moses's sister found out about his intentions and begged him to make the extra trip over the pass to find Moses and lead him to safety.

Martin showed Moses how to make his snowshoes more useful by altering their shape and attaching them only at the toe to reduce the amount of snow that collected on top. The next morning, despite Moses's malnourished condition, the two started out for the Yuba camp, crossing the summit successfully. After a few days they reached the other emigrants, who, although cold and hungry, rejoiced to see Moses alive and well. About the same time, a rescue rider from Sutter's Fort made his way to the Yuba camp, bringing food and horses. With this help the travelers were able to journey out of the snow to the welcoming valley below. At Sutter's Fort they rested and ate heartily and then split up for their various destinations. All his life Moses gratefully remembered the delicious food they were given, especially a "fine fat cow" that seemed like a feast to him.

Moses returned to his little cabin again in June to guard the wagons until they could be hauled over the pass to California. Most of the goods had been stolen, but in July oxen were brought to pull the wagons themselves across the summit.

Moses went on to the settlement of Monterey and worked as a store clerk. He stayed there for several years, selling goods to miners during the 1849 gold rush. His sister and brother-in-law moved to a farm near San Jose. In 1850 both of them died, leaving an infant son, so Moses moved to San Jose to take over the care of both their little child and their farm. Four years later he married Fanny Everitt, and over the years the couple had five children of their own, one of whom, Maggie, later helped Moses record the memoirs of his westward journey.

Moses lived and farmed near San Jose all his life. He died there in 1909, an elderly man who had never forgotten his grueling months in the high Sierras. One of his most prized possessions was an iron wagon wheel rim—a souvenir of the trip that nearly cost him his life, but instead taught him the qualities of self-reliance and perseverance. ▨

WOODPECKER SOUP
FOR SUPPER

The Story of Henry and John Ferguson

It was pitch-black when eleven-year-old Henry Ferguson opened his eyes. No moonlight silhouetted the dark forest that cold November night, and heavy clouds hid the stars. He strained his eyes in the utter darkness inside the covered wagon and listened intently. Something was prowling around outside, but he couldn't tell what. Stiffening with fear, he nudged his thirteen-year-old brother, John, and together the terrified boys listened to the rustling and snuffling on the ground below. Henry wished desperately for his father's solid, sleeping bulk beside him or his mother's reassuring soft breathing, but they were gone. Here in this wild land of northern California, he and John were alone. They buried their heads under the quilts and lay shivering until the prowler moved off into the dark woods.

The next morning they found the tracks of a large grizzly around the wagon.

It was 1849 when Henry and John started west from Iowa with their family. Their father, W. W. Ferguson, and their mother, Mary Ferguson, loaded their belongings and their seven children into two wagons and headed west with the thousands of other emigrants who made the dangerous trip that year. California, where the gold rush called irresistibly to people from all walks of life, was their destination.

John and Henry were the elder children. Then came Elizabeth (nine), Nancy (seven), Paris (five), Martha (three), and Amanda (one). The family joined a train of forty other wagons and about three hundred people near the present-day site of Omaha, Nebraska. The emigrants didn't hurry as they meandered up the Platte River and out onto wide plains, but they made good time. Young, vibrant, and enthusiastic, the company enjoyed the first part of the trip, relishing the new sights and the beauty of their surroundings. While the women sizzled bacon and made coffee over their campfires, the men took care of the stock animals, making sure they had plenty of water and grass and attending to an occasional sore hoof or raw shoulder where the yokes rubbed. Henry and John, like most children, were needed to help their parents, and their chores might have included herding the cattle, gathering buffalo chips for campfire fuel, or searching the riverbank for duck or goose eggs. After helping with the camp work, the boys were probably allowed to wade in the shallow river, hunt birds, or play games with the other children. Little did they suspect that after this pleasant beginning to their overland journey, its conclusion would challenge their family's strength and courage to its limits. Much later in life, Henry recorded his memories of the wagon trip, assisted in his recollections by his brother John.

The wagon train entered Pawnee country, and the group's captain, Reverend J. S. Kirkpatrick, was aware that the tribe was becoming less tolerant of the flood of emigrants overrunning its lands. He ordered that the wagons be corralled at night, which was done by driving them into a large circle and securing the tongue of

WAGON TRAIN SIMILAR TO THE ONE JOHN AND HENRY FERGUSON
TRAVELED WITH DURING THE FIRST PART OF THEIR JOURNEY WEST.
COLLECTION OF THE NEW-YORK HISTORICAL SOCIETY, #67962

each wagon beneath the rear axle of the one in front of it. The opening was closed with heavy chains. The cattle were driven into this makeshift enclosure and closely guarded as the travelers slept. Despite their careful measures, one moonless night Pawnees stampeded the cattle, riling the animals until they burst through the chains. On the third attempt, the tribesmen were successful in taking seven yoke of oxen, one of which belonged to the Fergusons. Enraged, several of the company's young men wanted to seek revenge, but the wisdom of the older men prevailed and the decision was made to hitch up the remaining teams and move through Pawnee country as quickly as possible.

Starting early each morning, the emigrant train traveled hundreds of miles up the Platte River. Now and then the travelers stopped and rested for several days while the men hunted bison and antelope, the women washed clothing in the silty stream, and the children frolicked in the long grasses. On Sundays the captain gave a sermon. Everywhere they saw evidence of the thousands of travelers ahead of them—trampled vegetation, dead oxen and horses, gouged river banks, muddy crossings, and discarded belongings.

It was then that cholera hit the party. The emigrants knew no cure for the dreaded disease, but after one woman died and others became violently ill, the company physician advised the travelers to break into four groups of ten wagons each to avoid further contact. All nine of the Fergusons escaped the terrible illness, which is now known to have been primarily transmitted by fecal contamination of food or drinking water.

They passed Fort Laramie in today's state of Wyoming and then Independence Rock, which they reached sometime in late August. Most emigrant trains attempted to reach Independence Rock in time to celebrate the Fourth of July, and the Ferguson's wagon party was nearly six weeks behind that schedule. They began to worry about their slow pace, especially since they knew that the high Sierra Nevada mountain range awaited them at the end of the journey. Snow in the mountains meant an impassable trail for the wagons, and no travelers wanted to be stranded on the harsh eastern slopes for the winter.

Once again cholera attacked the travelers on the Big Sandy River in today's southern Idaho, but still the Fergusons avoided it. One man died while the party pushed on, crossing a desert of deep sand near the Green River and ferrying the wagons across the rushing stream. Moving on, day after day, mile after mile, week after week, the travelers—now worn, tired, and dusty—finally reached the Humboldt River in present-day Nevada. Henry recorded that his father fished its clear waters and caught large trout, which was cause for celebration, since the children by then were weary of eating stale bacon.

The wagons wended their way through dry sagebrush that sent up its pungent aroma when crushed under the ironclad wheels. Taking the Lassen Trail, they finally reached the dreaded Sierra Nevada, but this most difficult obstacle—rugged mountains to cross with worn-out oxen—seems to have been conquered without much trouble. Henry's notes simply state that they wound their way "over the summit, out by Goose Lake, and on to the head waters of the Pitt River." After days of moving down the Pitt, they came to the upper reaches of the Feather River and neared the long-awaited California gold camps.

The emigrants by then were reduced to two families traveling together, the Fergusons and the Alfords, and were only about fifty miles from the Sacramento River Valley settlements. They had been on the trail for seven hard months, and their spirits were flagging. The animals were doing poorly, the weather was gray, and a cold autumn wind whistled through the thick pines. One evening the Alfords went on ahead and the Fergusons drove behind, traveling until long after dark in the attempt to reach a stopping place known as Bruff's Camp for the night. There a crackling fire and plenty of savory roast venison prepared by their traveling companions greeted them. After the hearty meal, the tents were pitched and everyone fell into an exhausted sleep.

Near midnight a storm arose. With tornadolike winds, it ripped through the treetops, "twisting the trees in its fury . . .," Henry later recalled. It was then the travelers met with disaster. The old oak under which the two families were sleeping was uprooted and fell heavily on their tents. Four of the Alford family were killed or fatally injured and three of the younger Ferguson children were hurt. Frantic and distraught, the survivors begged the inhabitants of Bruff's Camp for help. The camp doctor came quickly along with some of the others, and while the doctor worked to help the injured, the men dug a deep grave for the Alford men. Joseph Goldsborough Bruff, an emigrant leader after whom Bruff's Camp was named, helped with the rescue.

Henry and John were most worried about their nine-year-old sister, Elizabeth, who had internal injuries and couldn't be moved for several days. To add to the trouble, snow fell until it covered the oxen's forage. In their exhausted state several of the cattle died. When the Fergusons finally determined it would be safe to travel, they struggled downhill a few miles until they were below the snow line. There more of the cattle died and the Fergusons abandoned one of their wagons. The family knew the gold camps were near, but they were in peril. Fortunately an earlier traveler who had also been forced to leave a wagon behind returned to retrieve it with fresh oxen. He invited the Fergusons to load a few of their belongings and the hurt children into his wagon and let his oxen pull them to the settlements. This they did, leaving Henry and John behind to guard the remaining Ferguson wagon and its load.

Alone in the wild forests of northern California, the two boys had very little to eat, but they had their guns and plenty of surrounding game. They slept in the wagon at night because of the bears that prowled the woods, and they hesitated to venture too far from camp even to hunt. John recalled:

> We were compelled to eat Woodpeckers, so we thought a soup made of them would be fine. We cooked them and made a search in the waggon for something to thicken the soup, and all we could find was about half-a pound of dried peaches. So, we cooked them in the broth and proceeded to eat, but in a short time two boys were about as sick as they could possibly be, throwing up all that was in them, and suffering horribly.

Weak and desperately hungry, the two decided to shoot a deer. With a careful plan, they ventured a mile or so away from camp, working together and hunting until they were successful. Dragging the animal back to camp, they began cooking the liver, but being ravenous, couldn't wait until it was ready. They ate it while it was still half raw, and once again became violently ill. It wasn't until the next day that they could thoroughly roast some venison and have a satisfying meal.

Heavy rains made it nearly impossible for the boys' father to return to get them, but after two weeks he was able to cross the swollen streams that lay between them. Riding on horseback, he was a welcome sight to the lonely boys, and he brought a big loaf of bread their mother had baked for them. But the streams were too high and the roads too muddy to move the wagon and all their belongings, so John and Henry had to stay for another week. By then, much to the boys' relief, Mr. Ferguson could get through with teams to pull the wagon to the settlements. The family spent the winter in a small house on a cattle ranch while Mr. Ferguson worked to earn their lodging and food.

In the years that followed their arrival in California, the family moved several times. The children's father found work in the lumber camps, and he and Mrs. Ferguson also started a boardinghouse in Marysville. At one point Mr. Ferguson became ill, so the children helped support the family by selling homemade candy to the gold miners. Candy, a luxury in that primitive setting, sold for "enormous prices," Henry recalled.

In 1852 the family moved to the mining country in Yuba County. There in the foothills of the great Sierra Nevada, they made their home for several years, mining and again running a boardinghouse. Two more children, Mary and William, were born. In 1857, the Fergusons relocated to Sonoma County and settled in Alexander Valley. It was their final home.

John and Henry lived long lives, as did some of their siblings, including Elizabeth, their sister who was so badly hurt when the tree fell on their tent. When John was eighty-two and Henry was eighty, the two collaborated on remembering and recording their trip west, a journey they called "a seemingly impossible undertaking. . . ." With thanks to their remarkable parents and to the God who saw them through to California, they dedicated their work, written in Henry's "aged shaky writing," to the offspring of the Ferguson family. ▦

Provisions to the Rescue

The Story of Octavius M. Pringle

Fourteen-year-old Octavius M. Pringle huddled under the low, sweeping boughs of an immense fir tree, trying to ignore the utter blackness and vast wilderness surrounding him. The night was wet, but under the tree where he had spread his blankets the ground was dry. An owl hooted in the distance, and nearby coyotes answered, sending their hair-raising, eerie howls into the darkness. Alone and frightened, Octavius pulled his worn blanket over his head, wishing for his family miles back on the trail and wondering if he would ever reach them safely with the provisions he'd ridden ahead to find—provisions that could save their lives.

Octavius had set off for Oregon with his family on April 15, 1846. At first he thought a wagon journey west would be a frolicking good time filled with adventure and a chance to see the world. Little did he suspect how the immense hardships ahead would threaten his family—and that his own courageous actions could mean the difference between life and death for them.

It was sixty-five years later when Octavius wrote down his memoirs of the trip. By then he was a gifted writer who added his reminiscences to his father's detailed diary of the trip. These accounts, and the letters of other family members, documented the Pringle family's trip west.

Back in Missouri, where they would begin their long journey, the Pringles (Virgil and Pherne Pringle and their several children) were joined by Octavius's grandmother, sixty-six-year-old Tabitha Brown, and a large group of other wagon travelers. Octavius loved to watch the long wagon train as it snaked its way across the prairie and along the shining rivers, winding gracefully amid the native grasses on the trail. The white canvas wagon tops, not yet dirty with the dust of the miles, snapped in the fresh breeze, and the spring rains brought the fragrance of damp earth and budding wildflowers.

Octavius and the other boys took time from herding the spare stock behind the wagons to wade in the cool creeks and enjoy the spring sunshine on their shoulders. Always hungry from the fresh air and exercise, they gathered around the campfires in the evenings, eagerly relating the day's events and eating tin platefuls of their mothers' biscuits and beans.

Before long, the travel lost its novelty, and the days became monotonous. Day after day the oxen plodded along, covering only ten to twenty miles from morning until night. Cold, unpleasant winds chilled the boys to the bone, and icy rain and hail beat down on them. A young girl traveling with her parents died, and the train halted for her burial. Octavius remembered the "grave and anxious expressions upon the countenance of parents and elders of the company."

The waving Nebraska grasslands disappeared behind them as the wagons got closer to Fort Laramie in today's state of Wyoming. By then it was June, and the weather was warmer. The muddy trail turned to dust. Grit roiled up behind the oxen and the huge iron-clad wagon wheels. The boys behind the wagons were covered with fine tan powder that settled on their sweaty faces and found its way into their eyes and mouths.

This was Sioux country, a beautiful territory that offered landmarks like the stark Chimney Rock and Scott's Bluff. It was unlike anything the emigrants had ever seen. Octavius undoubtedly marveled over the countless bison, the prairie dog towns that were scattered over the grassland and the many plants that were entirely foreign to him. No doubt he learned to watch the vast sky for the violent thunderstorms that let loose cracks of earsplitting thunder and nearby flashes of the most brilliant lightning he had ever seen. When they reached Fort Laramie, the party stopped and held a feast for what Octavius's father called their "Sioux brethren," smoking a peace pipe and offering them powder, lead, and tobacco.

Then the travelers pushed on, encountering deep sand, wind, and uneven rocky ground. Soon mountains appeared in the distance—the Wind River Range—and the altitude was high enough that the travelers found frost on their belongings on July Fourth. Octavius saw beaver and mountain sheep when he rambled away from the wagons with the other boys.

As the land got more rugged, the emigrants and oxen worked harder to cover the terrain as quickly as possible. Too many delays meant that snow would fly before they reached Oregon, stranding them in some cold, unknown wilderness. But broken axles, worn-out animals, and a rough road meant whole days spent resting and repairing wagons. As the party tried its best to make good time, they began to worry about reaching Oregon's Willamette Valley— their long-sought destination—before blizzards stopped them.

Near Fort Hall in today's state of Idaho, they met a scout who encouraged them to try a new route that promised to be easier and faster than the existing trail. The Pringles and some of the others in the party were persuaded to turn south on the California Trail and from there attempt the newly discovered Applegate Trail, which led into Oregon from the south. It was a decision they would sorely regret.

The Applegate Trail, despite its discoverers' good intentions, began with a fifty-mile desert, far south of their destination, that tried the oxen's stamina and weakened them for the days ahead. Mr. Pringle's diary, which told of each day's progress, became terse and grim, and he used the words "barren," "heavy pulling road," "jaded teams," and "water bad for drinking." After a miserable crossing, the party pressed on toward the mountains. There the trail became so rough in places that the wagons were virtually stopped while the men hacked their way through dense undergrowth. September gave way to October. Exhausted, discouraged, and facing a nearly impossible route, the emigrants began to run out of food. Octavius remembered:

> . . . with provisions so nearly exhausted that every one was on short rations, with many members of the company buried in unmarked graves by the wayside and every few days adding new graves to the number, with those who survived hungry, weak, travel worn and discouraged, . . . with winter storms beating upon us, we reached the southern border of the Territory of Oregon. . . .

The travelers knew they were in extreme danger and still had many miles yet to go. There was no fort nearby to replenish the food supply. Octavius's father tried to shoot game, but his arms trembled from hunger and fatigue, and he could not hold his rifle steady enough to aim. The oxen were too exhausted to work, so many of the wagons, some still filled with the emigrants' belongings, were left behind. It was cold, and the travelers were miserable as they watched some of their companions die along the way. "The extremity had now come with famine and starvation staring us in the face," wrote Octavius.

But Octavius was young and still somewhat strong. In desperation, his family made a difficult decision. He would take the only horse the party had left and travel three days ahead to a depot where food from the faraway settlements had been collected to help desperate emigrants still on the trails. A couple of young men the party had met, who were traveling through on their own, would go with him as far as the depot. Then Octavius would join other travelers returning his way and accompany them back to his family.

The first part of the trip went according to plan, and Octavius reached the depot safely with his temporary companions. He loaded as many sacks of dried peas and wheat flour as his worn and skinny horse could carry and prepared to return to his distressed family. But then the plan went awry; there was no one to accompany him on the return trip. Thoughts of the difficult forty-mile-long wilderness trail, Indians, and wolves crowded into Octavius's young mind as he realized he must travel back alone. He wrote:

> You may well imagine the disappointment and dreadful fear that came over this boy of 14 years when it was known that his return trip must be made alone. . . . But with undaunted courage and many misgivings he resolved to show no cowardice and thinking of parents, brothers and sisters who might be suffering for food resolved to make the attempt.

When morning came Octavius set out on foot, leading his packhorse. It was a gray, drizzly day, and the forest was foggy and dark. He was nervous and jumpy, especially when he found a large set of fresh bear tracks preceding him up the trail. It wasn't long before he came across the bear itself, but despite Octavius's startled fear, the animal only lumbered off into the woods. All day, he hurried through the wilderness, watching and listening for the next danger, which seemed to lurk behind every boulder and tree, and praying to God for safety. Dusk came, and he was tired and hungry but too frightened to stop. However, the fear of losing the trail in the darkness made him set up camp under the drooping boughs of a large fir. It was there, protected from the rain, that he spread his blankets on the dry ground and drifted into an uneasy sleep, only to be awakened by the yipping of coyotes. As soon as the wild howling subsided, he heard the crashing and heavy breathing of some large creature in the undergrowth. With heart pounding, he jumped to his feet, hauled the precious peas and flour into the thick fir branches, and spent the rest of the night roosting high above the ground.

In the morning he ate a cupful of flour and cold water and set off again. The thought of spending another night like the last made him vow to keep walking until he reached his family's wagons, no matter how long it took. Late in the afternoon he came to an Indian camp beside the trail. Fearful, but unable to escape detection, he approached.

Women and children greeted him. They spoke a few words of English and welcomed him to their camp, letting him know that the men were out hunting deer and would return soon. "They took care of my things and myself as though I had been a brother, and there was nothing to fear from them . . .," Octavius recalled later. When the men returned with venison, the Indians boiled some of the delicious meat for him and prepared more for him to take with him the next day. They offered him a warm, dry part of a tepee, where he slept soundly until morning, and the next day they traded a whole carcass of deer for some powder, lead, and caps.

When Octavius set out again, he was laden with food for his family. "They treated me as royally as though I had been a prince ...," he wrote gratefully in his memoirs.

Certain that he still had miles to cover, Octavius hurried along as best he could. It was near noon when he heard someone coming toward him, urging on a delinquent ox. The voice was his brother Clark's, and a short way behind him were the rest of the Pringle family and their two wagons inching up the trail. Immense relief and thankfulness swept over Octavius as he greeted his loved ones and gave them the simple foods he had brought to save their lives, which were immediately made into a feast. Mrs. Pringle vowed amid tears of joy and thankfulness that she would never again let any of her children travel ahead alone. She had been tortured by thoughts of Octavius being mauled by wild animals or harmed by Indians. The family said fervent prayers of thanks for his safe return and for the supplies that replenished their strength.

They pressed on until they came to the Indian camp where Octavius had been treated so kindly. There they stopped for three days to rest the oxen. Mr. Pringle and Octavius, who were both skilled shoemakers, spent the time with their cobbler kit repairing and making shoes for their family and for one of their Indian hosts, who traded them more venison for the leather footwear.

With renewed courage, the Pringles crossed the Calapooia Mountains and dropped into the Willamette Valley. Seventy-five miles still remained to the small settlement of Salem, which was their destination, and the family was once again stalled. This time the oxen had entirely given out and could travel no farther. Just as the outlook was its most grim, one of Octavius's uncles, who had migrated to Oregon earlier and had heard of their plight, came to their rescue from the north, bringing supplies and hired pack-horses.

CLARK S. AND OCTAVIUS PRINGLE IN THEIR
LATER YEARS.

It was Christmas Day 1846 when the Pringles arrived at Salem, footsore, weak, and tired, but thankful to be alive. As soon as they found housing, the weather turned cold, and Octavius wrote that "we would surely have perished in such weather had we not reached shelter." Grateful to God and each other, the family began their new life in the lush and beautiful valley.

Octavius lived his long life in the Oregon country he helped settle. In 1874 he moved from Salem to central Oregon, where he lived near Prineville. Pringle Falls on the Deschutes River is named after him. He often looked back on his family's treacherous overland journey and the peril on the Applegate Trail, from which he rescued them by his own bold, solitary boyhood expedition. Never did he forget the dense, dripping forest with its dark nights, the generosity of the Indians who helped him, or the intense joy at being reunited with his family.

Octavius Pringle died in Portland in 1914 when he was more than eighty years old, leaving two daughters, a son, and a host of relatives who, along with Octavius himself, had become some of Oregon's foremost early pioneers. ▣

ABOVE AND BEYOND THE CALL OF DUTY

The Story of Welborn Beeson

Sixteen-year-old Welborn Beeson held his breath. The Skunk River bottomland just west of the Mississippi had been hard enough to cross. The ironclad wagon wheels and the oxen's hooves sank into the black mud as though it were molasses. What came next looked even more daunting. Welborn and his parents stared at the fragile half-mile-long pole bridge built tentatively across the rushing Skunk, wondering if it could hold their two-thousand-pound wagons and heavy oxen. Others had obviously crossed it before them. Carefully they ventured out onto the rickety structure, which shook and swayed under the weight. Welborn tried not to look at the brown waters rushing by twenty feet below. It seemed as if any second, he, his parents, the oxen, and the loaded wagons would go plunging into the current. Still, it was the only means across this river, and there was no choice but to continue.

The half mile seemed an eternity, but the bridge held. Eventually the wagons were safely across, much to the family's relief, and the small emigrant party was on its way through the timbered lowlands again. Welborn wondered about the trail ahead and about other unknown dangers that awaited them as they made their slow way across the overland trail to Oregon.

Some wagon travelers started west on a moment's whim, but the Beesons (Welborn and his English-born parents, Ann and John) took more than a year to prepare for the trip. They sold their Illinois farm and arranged for two covered wagons and the livestock to pull them. During the long evenings, they read John Frémont's *Narrative Across the Rocky Mountains,* a well-known western guidebook, aloud to each other. As the weeks passed, they bought items they would need on the long, treacherous journey: an axe, guns, a churn, a tin washtub, and a sheet iron stove for outdoor cooking, among other necessities. They hired a teamster, readied their sleeping tent, made candles, saved seeds, and preserved foods. Last, they auctioned the belongings they would not be able to take along and said sad good-byes to their neighbors, church acquaintances, and friends. On the cold morning of March 16, 1853, they set off on their long journey.

Welborn took along his precious pencils and pocket-size notebook. For two years he had been keeping a diary, and as the family started west he continued to write down the events and details of his life. Rain or shine, in health or illness, he told his family's story so carefully and thoroughly that today his diaries are important historical documents.

Almost immediately they encountered heavy rain and difficult, muddy roads, but the downpour didn't seem to bother the Beesons. Welborn reported in his matter-of-fact way that they put hay in their sleeping tent and got a good night's sleep anyway. The weather improved as the group traveled over the beautiful prairie and camped at small towns and homes along the way. Ten days later they crossed the majestic Mississippi using a steam ferry to get their belongings—including the livestock—to the far shore.

Then they struck out for the Missouri, dodging mud holes, stumps, and hills, and reaching the "jumping off" places (departure points for the overland trails) near the end of April. After a short delay, they ferried to the western side of the Missouri and set out with a small group of others to cross the plains.

Days of slow travel followed, and the Beesons soon left their companions. Welborn's diary does not tell why, but it seems likely that his family was trying to make better time. They joined another group up ahead—a party of seven wagons headed for Oregon's Rogue River Valley. This energetic company often started their day's journey before five in the morning and covered more than twenty miles a day as they continued up the Platte River. After weeks of travel, they reached Fort Laramie, visible across the swollen waters of the Platte in today's southeast corner of Wyoming, but the river was so high they could not cross over to trade or mail their letters.

Near Laramie in early June, Welborn reported that he was "very sick with the mountain feaver." Even though he was weak and tired, he wrote daily in his diary, telling of the wild geese they saw and an Indian village where he bought a bison skin for four dollars. He stumbled feverishly along on foot beside the train until his mother saw him lagging and insisted he ride Sallie, the family's favorite horse. Young and otherwise healthy, Welborn soon recovered and in a few days was again scouting ahead and hunting antelope. He remarked on the beauty of the prickly pear in bloom and the proximity of snow-capped Laramie Peak.

Spring gave way to summer as the party moved into dry countryside. Pushing on, they left the Platte River and crossed the Divide to the Sweetwater drainage. There the grass was poor, the roads were sandy, and Welborn scrawled in his diary that the sun was intense. Always concerned about the animals, he reported that they encountered "alkali" water, which was poisonous for live-stock. Grass for grazing dwindled until there was "nothing but sagebrush in sight." On one occasion, they left the road and made a six-mile detour to the nearby mountains, where abundant grass was found. There the hungry cattle grazed too much and delayed the party when they became sick. The emigrants poured melted lard down their throats as a remedy, and, after a pleasant after-noon that Welborn spent enjoying a patch of snow, they were on the road again.

It was then that Welborn experienced what must have been the low point of the trip. Not only did his mother get so sick she couldn't get out of the wagon (it is possible that she, too, had mountain fever), but Welborn also witnessed an incident undoubt-edly disturbing to a young man with his steady, loyal tempera-ment. Two men of the party—a drover and a teamster—had a heated argument that ended when the drover struck the teamster, Charly, from behind and knocked him unconscious. Although a doctor came, possibly from another wagon train, there was noth-ing that could be done, and Charly died of his injuries a few days later. The drover fled.

The company continued, and Ann Beeson made a slow recovery from her illness. By June 20, she was able to get out of the wagon again, just in time to cross South Pass, the gentle slope over the Continental Divide. Welborn's diary mentions passing a village of Snake Indians and a couple of trading posts. He was assigned night guard duty often and took the responsibility seriously, watching over the cattle and the camp while the others rested. In his worn notebook, he frequently reported that a few of the horses or cattle had wandered off and it was his job to find them.

Although he didn't complain in his diary, he did seem bothered by the thousands of mosquitoes that tormented the travelers on this stretch of trail. And he mentioned they were "all sleepy enough" after plodding one long night across forty miles of desert so they could travel in the cool darkness. They reached the Green River in present-day southern Idaho, where they refreshed themselves and the cattle. Frenchmen living in wigwams nearby ran ferryboats across the Green for a fee, and the Beesons paid $21.50 to transport their two wagons, horses, and small herd of cattle across.

With his usual concern, Welborn reported that his father had slipped and fallen on the sharp edge of the wagon bed, hurting himself internally. "He cannot get around," his son wrote, wondering if the injuries would affect his father for life, although no further mention of the problem appears in Welborn's trail diary. Of necessity, the party moved ahead. The landscape was mountainous, making travel more treacherous, especially the steep descents where it seemed the wagons would overturn. By then, Welborn wrote, they had traveled 1,500 miles.

They celebrated July Fourth by firing pistols and guns into the air, then moved on the next day to Idaho's Soda Springs, where they mixed cream of tartar and sugar with the bubbling spring water for a delicious drink. Turning south, the party took the California Trail along the Humboldt River in today's state of Nevada. Their plan was to turn north again at Lassen Meadows and follow the Applegate Trail into southern Oregon. Fish were abundant, supplementing the travelers' diets, but the oxen were not faring well. Several died along the trail or had to be left behind because they could no longer travel.

It was hot along the Humboldt. Blue-green willows lined the riverbanks, where there were bullfrogs, snakes, snails, and lizards. The river was swift and deep, but the dusty travelers swam in the refreshing water in spite of the current. On July 22, 1853, Welborn celebrated his seventeenth birthday.

He seemed intrigued by the information that filtered back to the train that the famous Kit Carson was traveling a few days ahead of their party on the same trail, driving a large flock of sheep. Indeed the wagon travelers did see a few stray sheep that had been left behind. Hundreds of dead cattle and horses lay in the trail, "until the road is almost blocked up," Welborn wrote in his diary. This is where the Beesons' careful planning and preparation for the trip was fruitful, since they were able to continue traveling with few casualties. Welborn and his father constantly watched out for the livestock, trading weak ones, shoeing them with leather, or giving them lard when they faltered.

Fellow travelers came and went, but the group stayed fairly small and constant. In early August the Beesons camped with a large company near the Applegate Trail turnoff. Welborn enjoyed their fiddle music and a "grand dance" that was held under the sparkling stars on the black desert.

More cattle died, and another all-night desert crossing demanded the travelers' attention. After that, they trudged mile after mile on the Applegate Trail through the hot and arid land in today's northern Nevada, eating hares and sage hens and hopping from coffee-brown watering hole to sparse spring. By mid-August, the train had reached today's northeastern corner of California where the terrain was again rough and mountainous. From the top of a steep pass, the emigrants could see beautiful Goose Lake ("full of water fowl of every description," Welborn remarked) sparkling in the distance. The road was rocky, and heavy timber or fallen logs sometimes blocked their way, but the tired travelers realized they were nearing their destination, so they pushed through the undergrowth and reached Klamath Lake in southern Oregon. Hilly, stony roads followed, and Welborn wrote, "We cannot hardly find a place to lay down without rolling down into the gully."

It was August 30, 1853, when the Beesons reached their destination near today's site of Talent, Oregon. Weary but healthy, they bought a farm with a two-room log house and began at once to work the land. Hard, physical chores were so much a part of Welborn's life that while he was "resting from the long journey," he helped make one thousand clapboards for a stable roof, broke the ground for crops, and hauled and split rails.

It was a time of unrest between the native peoples of the Rogue River Valley and the new settlers. Violence broke out, and the white settlers were intent on subduing the Indians by any means possible. Welborn's father, however, was not among them. Back in Illinois he had helped runaway slaves escape, and in Oregon he spoke out against the white settlers' brutal treatment of the Indians, much to the rage of his fellow newcomers. One dark night he was forced to flee his new home in fear of his life, and he had to stay away for several years until hostility toward him subsided. Today he is remembered as the first civil rights worker in Oregon.

Care of the farm fell to Welborn, who, with his typical diligence and ambition, worked day and night to support himself and his mother, chopping timber, plowing fields, planting, and harvesting. As the years passed, he also offered his services to the Oregon Militia. In 1866, thirteen years after his family arrived in Oregon, he married Mary Catherine Brophy, whom he fondly called "Kate," and with whom he had eight children, four sons and four daughters.

There in the beautiful green hills of southern Oregon, Welborn Beeson lived out his life, farming and raising his family. He died of heart failure in his fifty-seventh year. Kate and all eight of his children survived him.

Welborn Beeson's life was filled with love and hard work and great responsibility. He is recognized today as one of the important

WELBORN BEESON WITH HIS WIFE, MARY CATHERINE.
SOUTHERN OREGON HISTORICAL SOCIETY, NEG. 15991

founding fathers of the southern Oregon valleys. Year after year he faithfully kept his journal, recording the details and important events of his life. His small notebooks filled with his distinctive handwriting are now old and fragile, but they offer many insights into life in early Oregon. Even more important, they bring to life the respectful, uncomplaining, reliable farm boy who wrote down, probably by moonlight or flickering firelight, the daily events of his trip across the overland trail. ▦

IF I SHOULD DIE
BEFORE I WAKE

The Story of Elisha Brooks

Elisha Brooks peeked out from beneath the covered wagon, trembling with fear. Pawnees, plenty of them, had blocked the trail and forced his family's wagon company to stop. Convinced he was going to die at the hands of these tribesmen about whom he had heard so much, he squeezed his eyes shut and prayed for protection. Even at eleven years old, Elisha knew of the great Pawnees, and he drew back under the wagon wheels as best he could. When no sounds of battle reached his ears, he opened his eyes, thoroughly relieved to see that the native people held out their hands in peace. Elisha knew at once that he was safe and that his family could continue its long journey west that spring of 1852.

Two years earlier Elisha's father had gone to California in search of better health and gold. His health did improve, and he wrote to his family, wishing they were with him, so they could all make their home in that warm, promising land. Shortly after receiving the letter, Elisha's mother, Eliza Brooks, decided that despite the many dangers, she and the couple's six children would make the grueling trip. Within two weeks she had written her husband of her plans, filled a covered wagon with provisions, hired a man to drive the four yoke of oxen, and, with her family, joined a small company leaving Michigan for California.

The children were young. Besides Elisha and his twin brother, Elijah, there were boys ages four, six, and nine, and a girl of thirteen. Despite their youth their mother was eager to leave the mosquito-infested swamps around their Michigan home and begin the daunting 2,800-mile journey. Much later in his life, Elisha wrote down the details of their remarkable trip as a memoir for his grandchildren. His writings were filled with humor that served to soften the story of an otherwise treacherous westward journey. Perhaps the most lighthearted of his anecdotes told of a day on the trail when he discovered the hidden supply of dried apples: "From my experience I can recommend dried apples as an economical diet; you need but one meal a day; you can eat dried apples for breakfast, drink water for dinner and swell for supper."

As soon as the family set out, the weather turned bad. The children slogged through mud and huddled around the sheet-iron stove in the wagon trying to stay dry and warm amid late-spring blizzards. Once they fled to a nearby farmhouse to avoid freezing to death when the temperature dropped to nineteen degrees below zero. During another storm Elisha awoke in the night to find that the camping tent had blown down upon him and his brother. Their beds were floating in rainwater. Elisha reported that they climbed into the crowded wagon, where they "stood up in wet misery until morning, then plodded on our joyful way."

Just after crossing the Mississippi on a small ferry, all six children came down with the measles. Camped on the snowy ground, the family was delayed a week while they recovered. At last they were able to continue, and soon they arrived at Council Bluffs, a starting point for the overland trails located on the Missouri River.

There they heard stories of the immense dangers they were facing—tales of hardship and treachery almost beyond belief. Many travelers changed their minds about undertaking the trip, including the Brooks' hired teamster, who was managing their wagon. Deserted on the banks of the great Missouri, Mrs. Brooks was resolute. "She crossed the river and pushed out into the mysterious West, into the teeth of the unknown terrors—alone with her six little children," Elisha wrote. Her resolve seemed to waver when soon afterward they stopped within view of a Pawnee camp, but her prayers and her children—innocently confident that they could manage—spurred the family on.

The road was physically demanding and grew harder with each passing day. The family lacked the strength to keep up with its demands on their own so after a short time they joined an overland party traveling nearby. The group was made up of renegades Elisha called "roughs," but they helped the Brooks drive their wagon and offered the protection of a larger group. Despite the family's distaste for the men's characters, they continued west. Elisha was infuriated when their new driver killed his mother's precious laying hens and feasted on them with his companions.

All around them green prairie grass blew like ocean waves in the fresh wind, and flowers bloomed in profusion. Huge herds of bison roamed freely over the seemingly endless plains. At times the bison would stampede with a sound like thunder, once coming straight toward the emigrants' camp on the banks of the Platte River. The pioneers forced the rushing herd to veer aside slightly by waving their arms, shouting, and shooting guns, but at least one tent was flattened.

Along the trail, which followed the Platte through present-day Nebraska, were the frequent graves of earlier travelers who had succumbed to cholera. The Brooks family was able to avoid the terrible epidemic, but Elisha's party lost one man and a freight wagon to the currents of the river. As the trail wound farther from civilization, Elisha marveled, "Broken down wagons, harness, trunks, camp-utensils, mining machinery, dead animals in all stages of decay lined the road. . . ." All these were signs of the harried travelers ahead of them.

Tensions had been building for several years between the westward-bound emigrants and the native peoples of the Plains, with violence often the result. The wagon party was now in Sioux country, and Elisha was fearful of the warriors who sometimes followed the train. He welcomed the howling of wolves at night, since it meant the Sioux were not nearby. In his memoir Elisha mentioned that he thought that his bedtime prayers seemed likely to come true. Every evening he and his siblings folded their hands and whispered into the darkness, "If I should die before I wake, I pray the Lord my soul to take" and then wondered with childish fear if they would live to see the morning light.

Out on the Laramie Plains, the party encountered a band of one hundred Sioux lining both sides of the trail, a sight that was terrifying to young Elisha. To make matters worse, their teamster was "taken suddenly sick" and hid in the wagon. Eleven-year-old Elisha drove the oxen through the throng. Once again, despite his worries, the Sioux were friendly and interested in trading, and the family swapped pins for moccasins for each child. Mrs. Brooks traded a blanket and a pint of sugar for a pony.

As the trail meandered near the Rocky Mountains, Mrs. Brooks became more and more distressed with their rough companions. On July Fourth, when the group celebrated with a drunken brawl, she decided that she and the children would travel on alone. The teamster, who undoubtedly had been using the Brooks' food supply, was not pleased with the decision, but Mrs. Brooks paid him with blankets and provisions to leave. Elisha remembered that first dark night his family spent huddled alone in the wilderness, fully aware that six children and a woman traveling on their own were in true danger.

Homesick and troubled, they pushed on, the children commanding the oxen as the animals slowly "dropped by the wayside one by one." It was no wonder the stock animals were weak. With its slow pace, the Brooks family had fallen behind thousands of other emigrants that summer, and as a result, the rich grasses that had once flanked the trail were grazed away by vast numbers of livestock ahead. To make matters worse, clouds of grasshoppers had eaten the remaining vegetation, and the scarce water was often poisoned with alkali. If a wagon train overtook them, the tired family would attempt to join it and keep up, but their animals would soon falter, and once again they would be left behind.

It was during this trying time—near the Sweetwater River in today's state of Wyoming—that a party of migrating Crow Indians befriended the struggling family. Elisha's writings do not tell about their meeting or the circumstances surrounding this unusual occurrence, but the Crow obviously recognized the family's terrible vulnerability. They traveled with Mrs. Brooks and her children for a week or more and camped near them at night, offering their protection and company. Even at his young age, Elisha marveled at this, noting the colorful picture they painted together. Some of the Crow were adorned with fur robes, feathers, and beads, and carried babies in ornamented cradles, while others barely had rags to wear. Dogs and ponies carried their belongings. Along with them plodded the Brooks' remnant of a team of oxen, pulling a trail-worn covered wagon, a weary and bedraggled Mrs. Brooks, and her six dusty children.

Independence Rock loomed ahead, 190 feet high and half a mile

A SMALL WAGON PARTY, SIMILAR TO THE ONES ELISHA BROOKS
TRAVELED WITH, REACHES BESSEMER BEND—WHERE THE OREGON
TRAIL LEFT THE NORTH PLATTE RIVER FOR THE SWEETWATER.
NATIONAL ARCHIVES, NWDNS-57-HS-277

long, and there the children were overjoyed to find their father's name etched among hundreds of others in the stone. The family carved their names with his before striking out again. In the hot August sun, their oxen continued to die, and it wasn't long before the milk cows had to be pressed into service. Soon they too stumbled and died and had to be left by the wayside. The few remaining animals were sickly and weak, but there was no choice but to press onward. The family cast out all their possessions except the "absolute necessities" and chose a lighter wagon from the many discarded on the trail. Fearful of the Blackfeet and Shoshone who watched from the ridge tops, the Brooks family joined a strong wagon party for that stretch of the trail. This time they were able to keep up as day after day they crept across the dry countryside, turning south on the California Trail.

Provisions were getting scarce as the family inched through today's northern Nevada. Perhaps it was Elisha who baited a pin hook with grasshoppers and caught the few small fish he mentions in his memoirs. But near the sink of the Humboldt River, they made the "last cup of flour into flapjacks" and ate the last of their bacon. Survival looked uncertain, and Elisha's memoirs about the hardships there lacked the gentle humor that characterized his earlier writing. Only two oxen remained, and the children were so exhausted and thirsty that they no longer complained of hunger. Ahead lay the daunting Sierra Nevada range, perhaps the most rugged stretch of the long journey.

Plodding desperately along, they noticed a mule and rider approaching from the west. As he got closer, he began to look familiar. Astonishment and gratitude overtook them as they slowly realized the rider was their father, who had traveled three hundred miles from the Sacramento Valley to meet them. Mr. Brooks had just received their letter and, remembering his own perilous trip west, was alarmed for his family's safety. Heading east, he asked every person he saw until he met some travelers who knew of his family far back on the trail. Hurrying on, he finally found his wife and all six children, exhausted and weak but alive. Immediately, he added his mule to their team and replenished their food from supplies he had brought along. Together again, the family headed for the welcoming valleys to the west.

The trail took them through desert so long and dry that when the emaciated stock smelled the cool waters of the Truckee River—still a mile away—they "started on a staggering run and plunged into its cool depths," wrote Elisha, who, with his family, also joyfully bathed in the cool current. With their spirits high and their bodies somewhat replenished, they tackled the rugged mountains ahead. Here Elisha's writings were brief, describing in a few words the steep canyons, cliffs, and dense forests they navigated until they reached the difficult summit. From a rocky ridge at the top, they looked down upon the beautiful land of their dreams with immense thankfulness and relief. Then they slowly descended to their destination on the Feather River.

In a poignant note in his memoirs, Elisha paid tribute to the team of two faithful oxen that lasted thousands of miles and pulled the family's wagon through the final stretch of wilderness. His greatest admiration, though, was for his brave mother, who overcame great odds to cross the continent safely with her little family. She was a stalwart pioneer who gave up the "springs of her vitality," as Elisha put it, to help settle the new land. Exhausted from the journey's immense strain, Eliza Brooks died a few years later.

Settling in a rough mining town, Elisha helped his family survive by herding stock and delivering milk. He spent his teenage years studying in San Francisco and later became a teacher and then the principal of a school known for its excellent academics.

According to historical sources, he married and raised a family, and in 1904 he moved to the small California town of Ben Lomond, where he became an expert apple grower.

Perhaps one of Elisha's greatest contributions was the writing of his remembrances at the age of eighty-one. Without the memoirs of his overland trip, his family might have been among the many unsung pioneers whose westward journeys went unrecognized. With humor and insight, he preserved his memories of perhaps the greatest migration in the history of humankind—and told of his family's unlikely survival on the overland trail. ▦

BAREFOOT TOWARD ZION

The Story of Brigham H. Roberts

B
righam Henry Roberts trudged along the faint wagon tracks etched on the damp ground along the river. The early morning sky glowed gold and purple. Today the wagon train would ford the Platte, and Brigham couldn't wait to be first at the crossing. He had slipped silently from his uncomfortable, cold sleeping place on the ground and set out alone. No one would miss him, except perhaps his older sister, who was his traveling companion. With no parents along to watch over him, Brigham, at nine or perhaps ten years old, was responsible for himself.

Arriving at the great crossing at last, he found a clump of willows upstream where he could rest until the wagons caught up. He lay down, tired from his restless night and his long walk, and shut his eyes. By the time the wagons arrived, he was sound asleep. Nothing awakened him—not the teamsters shouting, the cattle bellowing, nor the wagons creaking as one by one they forded the river. When Brigham finally awoke, the last wagon was climbing the far riverbank. He was left behind on the shore, yelling to attract someone's attention.

The wagon train's captain, William Henry Chipman, was sitting on his horse watching the progress of his wagons when he heard

Brigham calling. Shouting back, he asked the boy if he could swim. Brigham hollered back that he could, so the captain instructed him to try the current. Brigham, knowing that he would be unable to stay afloat in his European iron-rimmed clogs and heavy coat, removed them and left them on the riverbank. Then, wearing only his old thin shirt and ragged trousers, he waded into the water.

The current swept the boy downstream as he swam, and Captain Chipman rode his horse into the water to help. Grabbing the captain's foot, Brigham held on as the horse swam for shore, and soon the man and boy were safely on dry land. The captain took his small horsewhip and, to teach the boy a lesson, slashed Brigham across the back of his threadbare pants. His coat and shoes stayed where he had left them on the opposite shore.

Brigham's teenage sister, Mary (whom he called "Polly"), had indeed missed her brother (nicknamed "Harry") and was terribly upset by his absence. She welcomed his return to the wagon train with joy and relief. Although the wagon trip to Utah Territory had not been in progress long, the two had already traveled halfway around the world together.

Born in England to Ann and Benjamin Roberts, the children were part of a family destined for separation. Their parents differed in many ways; one way was the strength of their convictions about their Mormon faith. According to Brigham's autobiography, which he wrote at the age of seventy-six, Mormon teachings became "a message of divine importance" to his mother. Brigham's father was less convinced. He was somewhat unstable and often absent from the family home, so when the call came for Mormon believers to gather to Zion—that promised land near the Great Salt Lake in America—Ann Roberts felt a strong need to go. Leaving her husband to his "intemperate habits," she found separate temporary homes for two of her children (Brigham, about age four or five, and

Mary), and taking her baby and young daughter, Annie, set off across the ocean. Her plan was to earn enough money in America to send for Brigham and Mary at a later date.

It was a sad and disturbing time for little Brigham. His foster family had problems of their own, and Brigham often made his bed under a tavern table while they drank and entertained themselves before returning to their "wretched home." More than once he ran away, only to be pursued and returned to his nightmarish situation. His one happy memory was that his foster mother read to him, usually from the Bible or books about Mormon church history. He found these times to be the highlights of his early childhood, and one of his greatest dreams was that he, too, could learn to read and write.

It was more than four years later, during the winter of 1866, when word was received that the two Roberts children should be sent to America. Boarding the *John Bright*, a sailing ship bound for New York with about one thousand passengers, Brigham and Mary left Liverpool and crossed the Atlantic, weathering storms and surviving the cramped, unhealthy conditions onboard. Malnourished, dirty, and ragged, the two set off with other Mormon emigrants to cross the continent. Zigzagging by rail and riverboat to Montreal and Niagara Falls, they then progressed through Chicago and arrived at a point just south of Council Bluffs on the Missouri— their jumping-off point for the Mormon settlement at Salt Lake City—on June 19, 1866.

There wagons and livestock awaited them, sent out from the settlers in Utah Territory to help their fellow believers reach the promised land. (Later in their lives, Brigham and Mary would repay the church's Perpetual Emigration Fund, donated money that made it possible for followers to make the trip from Europe to Salt Lake.) Young men were recruited to act as teamsters for the newcomers and sent from Zion as missionaries. It took nearly a month to outfit the wagons and divide them into companies. Brigham, his sister, and the other emigrants relished this chance to rest in the warm sunshine and fatten the livestock on the abundant grass. Being a child, Brigham had few responsibilities to prepare for the long trip ahead, and he spent his time swimming, fishing, and exploring the riverbank.

By mid-July, the wagons were ready for the trip, and the large company started west. Brigham and Mary were assigned to a wagon with two other families and were told they were to walk beside it during the trip. Brigham appreciated the imposing sight of the many canvas-covered wagons meandering along the trail under the blue prairie sky. The smell of dust, sage, manure, and campfire smoke filled the air. As the train wound its way along the Platte River, Brigham began to realize how ill-prepared he and Mary were for the overland trip. Their mother had sent handmade quilts to serve as bedding, a few items of warm clothing, and a small sum of money, but the teamster in charge of delivering these vital supplies never did so. After the crossing of the Platte where Brigham left his wooden clogs and his heavy coat on the riverbank, he had nothing but a thin, worn shirt and trousers.

Nights were the worst, for during most days the sun was warm. After sunset, the prairie winds were cool, and a chill descended from the dark, starry skies. Mary slept in the wagon with the rest of the women, but Brigham made his bed—without any bedding at all—on the damp ground under the wagon. Each night after retiring, Mary would slip him her flannel petticoat to use as a covering. He gratefully used it, although it was completely inadequate and he shivered through the nights under its thin protection.

Several incidents about the wagon journey stood out in Brigham's mind when he recorded his memoirs. He remembered clearly the day he and another young boy lingered behind the wagons picking yellow currants. When their caps were full, they turned to catch up to the train but were intercepted by three Indian men on horseback. When the boys attempted to go around them, the men blocked their way, looking sober. Brigham remembered his captain's words about the possibility of emigrant children being captured and was filled with "magnificent terror." Shaking, he gave a tremendous shout, dropped his capful of berries, and made a mad dash for the wagons. He and his friend were successful in getting back to the train and were surprised to hear loud peals of laughter from the Indians, who had frightened them only for a prank.

Another time at a difficult river crossing, Brigham disregarded the captain's command that everyone wade across so the animals would have less load to pull through the current. Looking around, he saw a young woman who was too frightened to wade climb stealthily into a supply wagon for a furtive ride across. Brigham, deciding that he too wanted to ride, climbed in beside her. To their dismay the wagon in which they rode was driven to the middle of the river and left there for the night while its stock animals were used again and again to pull other wagons out of quicksand. Brigham and the young woman were surrounded by a cargo of bacon, ham, and brown sugar, so they were not hungry, but when Brigham tried to climb down and cross the rest of the current on foot, the young woman pled tearfully for him to stay, since she was scared to spend the night alone in the middle of the river. He obliged, and the next day the wagon was pulled into camp with the others, where his frantic sister scolded him for disappearing. Brigham paid for the experience by losing the precious knife he had brought as a gift for his mother.

The trip was taking its toll on Brigham. The teamsters had shorn his thick black hair close to his head to get rid of the lice that had infested everyone on the ship from England. His bare feet were dirty, cracked, and bleeding from walking the long miles without shoes. When the wagons reached the dry country where cactus grew, sharp prickly pear thorns pierced his bare soles. Mary took time each evening to remove the thorns, crying tenderly at the pain she was inflicting on her young brother. (Later in the trip Brigham would find a pair of shoes on a dead man and appropriate them for himself, finishing the journey with their ill-fitting protection.)

His clothes were stiff with sweat, dirt, and sugar syrup. Brigham, along with the other children of the train, had discovered that sacks of sugar in the supply wagon had gotten wet and that sweet syrup was leaking through the cracks in the floorboards. Lying underneath, they enjoyed the sticky drips that flowed out onto their fingers and clothes. Brigham's shirt and trousers were further ruined when he hid in a molasses barrel to avoid trudging beside the wagons on a night march across a desert. His pants could stand up by themselves, he later said, but he had no change of clothing.

At noon stops and in the evenings, Brigham and the other boys searched the streams for swimming holes. One hot day the boys had cast their clothing on the streambank and jumped into the refreshing water when they saw Indians stampeding the cattle. Brigham and his companions rushed back to camp—leaving their clothing behind—to tell the captain. Captain Chipman saw the humor in their naked condition and sent them immediately back for their clothes. Then realizing the gravity of the situation, his first concern was to protect the emigrants. He quickly gave orders for the wagons to form a corral with the travelers and few remaining stock animals inside. Then he sent a small party of men out to retrieve the cattle. They found the herd heavily guarded near a large

Indian camp and were able to gather only a few strays that had been left behind and return to the train. One hundred of the company's strongest cattle were gone, as well as six or eight riding horses. The loss would severely hamper the rest of the trip.

Chimney Rock, the famous landmark in today's western Nebraska, rose to meet them. Brigham and Mary found the spot significant because their baby brother had died there on the trip west with their mother. Little Thomas, whom Brigham hardly remembered, was buried in a bread box between the spire of the towering rock and the Platte River.

The train moved on, its progress significantly slowed by the loss of the cattle. Aware that the journey would go on much longer than expected, the emigrants reduced the food rations so provisions would last the journey's duration. Despite the sacrifice, food ran out. Those men assigned to hunting doubled their efforts to bring in game, but meals were scanty. Summer was fading, the nights were cold, and one morning the wagons were covered with snow. Brigham, shivering under Mary's petticoat, wished heartily for a quick arrival at Salt Lake City.

They reached the Sweetwater and camped beside Independence Rock. Brigham remembered climbing the huge landmark, and he mentioned the beautiful view of the surrounding mountainous countryside from the top. The Sweetwater itself was so clear that it flowed in sparkling contrast to the muddy, turbid Platte through Devil's Gate and into unknown territory.

As they plodded through the seemingly endless wilderness, word of the stolen cattle and the near starvation reached Salt Lake City, and relief wagons were dispatched. Near the Big Sandy River, the two groups met. Aided by the renewed provisions, the wagon train "crawled its slow way along through the mountains and passed old Fort Bridger," Brigham later recalled. Day after long day, as the train dipped and climbed, Brigham watched the countryside for Echo Canyon, which the Utah teamsters had described as a place where echoes reverberated as if in answer to their calls. When they reached it at last, Brigham was enthralled when they sent their echoes "flying over the rugged cliffs that rose, perpendicularly for the most part, on the right hand of the stream."

Soon after Echo Canyon the travelers found the first of the long-awaited Mormon settlements. Staring at the crude dugouts and rundown log cabins that made up the town of Coalville, the emigrants were happy to see a gathering of their brethren, in spite of the primitive living conditions.

At last they neared the Salt Lake Valley. Early on the mid-September arrival day, the travelers quickly hitched up their teams and eagerly descended into the waiting city. The townspeople turned out to greet the large emigrant train, welcoming both the newcomers and the returning teamsters. While Mary hid in the wagon, desperately ashamed of her shabby condition, Brigham searched the crowd for their mother. When she finally appeared, Brigham wasn't certain he recognized her. She, too, seemed to take a few moments to recognize her trail-worn son with his chopped-off hair and threadbare clothes, but she knew Mary at once. There were tears of joy as the three were reunited.

A friend gave them a wagon ride to the settlement of Bountiful, where Brigham's mother owned a crude log cabin and sewed for a living. The cabin, Brigham noted, had a dirt roof over half of it and no roof over the other half. After greeting their sister, Annie, who had come west with their mother, Brigham was thoroughly bathed and scrubbed while Annie prepared a homecoming feast of flaky

MORMON EMIGRANT WAGONS TRAVEL THROUGH
ECHO CANYON CIRCA 1879.
NATIONAL ARCHIVES

white buttermilk biscuits with molasses. The little family, together at last, talked well into the night.

By the time he was eleven, Brigham had learned the alphabet in a private school held in a small house. Before long he was reading textbooks and chapters from the Bible. When a school was started by an old settler, Brigham became a student there and, showing an aptitude for academics, moved to the head of the class. He worked as a farmhand and later as a brick maker. In the meantime his mother remarried, and his new stepfather provided him with work driving teams of oxen for construction. Through the years and the jobs that followed, Brigham read constantly, introducing himself to the works of great writers and philosophers. Eventually he received a formal education from the University of Deseret (now the University of Utah).

Brigham lived a long, complex, and productive life. He became one of the leading intellectual writers and historians for the Church of Latter-day Saints and was one of its main theologians. His historical and theological writings, some published and some not, were abundant. In keeping with the belief of the time and place, he married three wives, with whom he had fifteen children. He spoke often in the great Tabernacle, where his clear voice resounded from the massive walls. With his colorful personality and unusual past, he sometimes found himself conflicting with other church leaders, but he was respected and well-liked. Among other accomplishments, he was elected to the United States House of Representatives. He was, however, denied his congressional seat because of controversy over his practice of polygamy. In his later years, he served as a chaplain in World War I.

As a young boy, Brigham H. Roberts was a small part of a great migration of Mormon followers. Fortunately he was a boy of

BRIGHAM H. ROBERTS.
THE CHURCH OF JESUS CHRIST OF LATTER-DAY SAINTS ARCHIVES, P 5653/1-3

uncommon resourcefulness and intelligence because, unlike most children journeying on the overland trails, he had no parents there to see that he followed orders, to wash and mend his encrusted clothes, and to ensure that he was warmly snuggled under thick quilts at night. As he trudged along the Mormon Trail to Zion on bare, blackened feet, little did he suspect that the independence, self-reliance, and quick wit he was forced to develop at such an early age would someday contribute to his remarkable adulthood. 图

To the Land of
Golden Shores

The Story of Charles Frederick True

Sixteen-year-old Charles Frederick True heard the cry of distress before he saw the accident. His mother and four-year-old sister, Carro, were riding on the dusty covered wagon's front seat as the oxen pulled it slowly along the Platte River that hot June morning. Charles himself was tramping beside the tired animals. When his mother cried out, he turned and saw little Carro, who had fallen, lying directly in the path of the huge, heavy wagon wheel. He watched in horror as the wheel rolled over her leg. In a flash he reacted, rushing to her and pulling her to safety before the larger rear wheel rolled over her head.

Although the little girl suffered a broken leg, Charles's quick action almost certainly saved her life. Their mother laid her on the ground on a makeshift bed while their father gathered his courage to set the leg himself, without experience or technical skill. The other travelers in their small wagon party clustered around to help while Charles led his distraught mother from the terrible scene. Then the grim volunteers approached the little girl, who by then was in shock, and, working carefully, set her leg with splints. Friends from another wagon gave up their comfortable spring seat so the child could have a cushioned ride inside the True family's wagon, where she would have to remain for several weeks.

It wasn't the only time that Charles was critically helpful during his family's overland journey. Many times he took on the responsibilities of an adult and contributed his youthful strength to getting his family through to California. All his life he vividly remembered his experiences, and in his later years he wrote them down. His inspiring and beautifully written work is entitled *The Overland Memoir of Charles Frederick True: A Teenager on the California Trail, 1859.*

It was May 1, 1859, when Ira and Elizabeth True and their four children started west from their home in Owatonna, Minnesota. Their manufactured covered wagon had a bluish-gray top, painted to make it waterproof, and it held all the family's belongings for the carefully planned trip to California. They traveled for five weeks in wet spring weather just to reach the jumping-off points for the overland trails along the Missouri River. Stocking up on supplies at Omaha and joining with seven other wagons for protection, they began their trek across Nebraska Territory on the north side of the slow and muddy Platte River. By 1859, ten years after the California gold rush and the year of the gold rush to Pike's Peak, the trail was a well-traveled road. Huge numbers of emigrants had preceded them, and the way was littered with belongings, old campfires, and dead animals, and it was marked with the graves of those who had perished along the way.

Charles remarked on the vast numbers of emigrants heading west that year and the lack of grass and feed for the oxen along the trampled and overgrazed routes. There were ferries at some of the difficult river crossings, where a hefty fee was charged for safe passage. The few forts along the route were used to the floods of emigrants by then, and their storerooms were stocked accordingly. Nevertheless, the way was long and hard. Mishaps, accidents, and illnesses were frequent.

Little Carro had her accident near the beginning of the trip. As Charles and his family continued up the Platte, they nursed her lovingly and helped entertain her as she lay strapped to the spring seat for safety. Eventually she was allowed to sit up, but always on the spring seat, so the wagon's rough jolting would not cause her leg to heal improperly.

Even Charles's pet dog, Prince, began to feel the trip's toll. As the miles passed, his enthusiastic romping turned into painful plodding as the pads of his feet wore down to a bloody rawness. One hot day he stopped beside the trail and began howling pathetically from the pain. Charles scooped him into his arms at once and set him into the wagon to ride. There Prince was delighted to find Carro and contentedly rode along with her for the next stretch of the trip.

From his memoir it is clear that Charles cared deeply about animals. He became attached to the three teams of oxen that faithfully pulled the wagon and was often concerned about their fatigue, thirst, calloused necks, and sore hooves, which eventually wore down to the painful quick. He had a fascination for wildlife and was especially intrigued by the huge herds of bison and the thousands of jackrabbits they encountered, as well as the coyotes, wolves, and wild sheep.

Early in June the party decided to try to reach Fort Laramie for July Fourth. They set a daily schedule for themselves, and, true to their goal, they arrived near the fort on the evening of July 3, 1859.

Here Charles and his party were disappointed, for the fort was located on a bluff across the North Platte River, which was raging with flood water and was nearly double its usual size. Although some of the men started to cross, their horses and mules held them back. The group was forced to spend the holiday on the wrong shore, realizing that their chance to purchase supplies, mail letters home, and socialize had come to nothing. Still, they were anticipating a day of rest and relaxation amid the beautiful surroundings.

That night was one of many when Charles was assigned to guard the livestock. He and his companion were a couple of miles from camp where the animals had been driven to find grass when his friend fell asleep, leaving Charles alone. As the nearby coyotes and wolves started their nightly chorus, the velvet black sky filled with thousands of stars. Bright moonlight silhouetted the dark hills, and the cattle rested. Charles later wrote:

> As I stood my solitary watch, I remember feeling almost overwhelmed by the vast loneliness and the strangeness of my position—a boy alone in the midst of a vast wilderness. Many times since then I have recalled that night . . . and I remember feeling an intense awareness of the beauty of the moonlit landscape and the wonder of my being there.

In the middle of the night, Charles woke his companion to take over the watch. Suddenly, without warning and seemingly without reason, the animals stood up and stampeded, racing away in the darkness. The two guards, distressed, confused, and without their horses, had to wait until dawn to find their way back to camp to report the misfortune. July Fourth, instead of being enjoyed in relaxation, was spent searching for the livestock on foot.

The animals were finally found and driven back to the wagons late in the day.

As the party pushed ahead, Charles and another boy swam the stock across the rushing waters of the north fork of the Platte to find grass. It was perilous work, but the two were assigned the job because of their light weight. They carried out the job and returned with the stock well fed.

On several occasions the wagon party was visited by Indians, but one time stood out in Charles's mind. The campers had labored through the hot morning to a beautiful midday picnic spot west of Fort Laramie, where there were plentiful green grasses and clumps of willows. They were relaxing in the shade when a Sioux warrior appeared without warning at the edge of their group. Immediately another arose from the grasses, and then another, until the True family and their friends were surrounded. But despite their surprise arrival, the Sioux were simply eager to talk and trade and smoke a pipe with the captain of the wagon train. Charles was fascinated by the visitors, whom he described as "splendid," "athletic," and "impressive." As the men talked, the chief announced that more Sioux would be passing through the area to fight the Pawnees. He also voiced concern over the flood of white emigrants and its effect on his people. "His calm manner of grave, almost sad dignity was characterized by a simple graciousness, as though of a nobleman of the empire—the Great American Desert," Charles observed.

The wagon travelers were nervous about the impending arrival of more Sioux and hurried on. The next evening as they set up camp, a large band of warriors on ponies appeared and surrounded them on all sides. Among them was a French Canadian trapper who spoke English. He advised the campers to move on even though night was fast approaching. The emigrants did not hesitate.

Hastily repacking their beds, tents, and smoldering cookstoves, they drove off. It was cold, windy, and rainy, and by the time they reached their next camp, everyone was exhausted. Early the next morning they were on the trail again, this time encountering another large group of war-painted Sioux. Although the women and children scrambled to hide in the wagons, the Sioux skirted the small wagon party and rode on their way.

At Devil's Gate, where the Sweetwater River cut through steep granite cliffs, Charles climbed to an overhang to enjoy the view of the rushing, tumbling rapids far below. He often took short side trips by himself, enjoying the scenery and the adventure. Near Devil's Gate he told of mountain sheep, and he often started out ahead of the wagons in the early mornings to examine and take imprints of the hundreds of wildlife tracks that appeared overnight in the dusty or muddy trail.

The small group climbed South Pass, the gradual ascent over the Rockies, and took the Sublette Cutoff to the Green River. There on the Green an accident occurred that very nearly cost Charles his life. The night guard, returning to camp with the livestock, neglected to unload his rifle. When it accidentally discharged, the slug slammed its way through Charles's cap, barely missing his head. Later he wrote about his deep gratitude that day to simply be alive.

The group then traveled north to the newly cut Lander Road. This relatively easy route took them to Fort Hall on Idaho's Snake River. Shortly afterward they reached the place where the Oregon and California Trails separated, and the True family and their friends began the long, arid trip south along the Humboldt River in present-day Nevada.

On one of his solitary treks (which Charles called "a desire to frequent out-of-the-way places and wander off ahead of our train, a habit I could not seem to resist") he was stopped in his tracks by the sudden and silent appearance of five large Humboldt wolves. The wagons were a mile behind him, but the wolves were only fifty feet away. He later remembered: "There we were, face to face. Their eyes? They appeared to be electrified. Their backs? The coarse, long hairs upon their spines were standing on end—every hair, I am positive. Yes, these glaring eyes, those razor-back spines and those hairs on end seemed to be enlarging every moment!" Terrified at the thought of their voracious appetites, Charles froze until the wolves, sniffing the air suspiciously, turned and walked away. Only then did he race back to the wagon's safety, and for a while his desire to explore alone was tempered by caution.

Charles wrote only briefly about the trip down the Humboldt River. He remembered plodding along for several weeks in deep alkaline dust, which covered the travelers and caused their skin to chap and bleed. Avoiding rocks in the trail, the weary travelers endured the oppressive late-summer heat. Charles remembered seeing mirages at this point in the journey, especially images of beautiful tree-lined lakes. Ahead lay the sink of the Humboldt— the place where the river disappeared underground—and the dreaded Forty Mile Desert scorching in the sun.

The True family had mixed feelings as they approached the sink, for although they were anxious about the dangerous desert crossing, they had also planned a reunion with Charles's uncle (his mother's brother) near the spot. Jefferson Tarr had gone to California in 1852 and established a ranch there. He planned to ride east, meet his sister and her family, and see them over the Sierra Nevada Mountains to the safety of his ranch.

Trouble plagued the family at the Forty Mile Desert. Although the cattle had held up well until then, the desert was by far the most stressful test of their endurance. Traveling all day in the terrible heat, the oxen were periodically given a small amount of the precious water carried in the wagon. To reach the desert's far side before the party perished it was necessary to travel steadily all night, as well, with only a brief rest at midnight when the animals were unhitched for a few moments. By the time the dust-covered, weary group reached the refreshing Carson River the next day, one of the True family's oxen had died from exhaustion. Then, as the family watched in disbelief, the remaining animals died. Charles remembered that they were "lying on their sides, dead, and bloated all out of recognition with their legs extending straight from their bodies." Distraught and sad at the fate of their faithful work animals, the family theorized that the oxen had found a pool of poisonous alkaline water at their midnight stop. The smallest ox and two milk cows were all that were left to pull the wagon over the mountains ahead.

Immediately the Trues discarded everything they could, including most of the wagon itself, keeping only the frame, wheels, and tongue. They tied their tent, a few belongings, and a frying pan to the wagon frame and set out for the Sierras, everyone walking except little Carro, whose leg was healing successfully but slowly. Their pace was so tedious that they had to say good-bye to their fellow travelers, who had no choice but to go on ahead.

At this discouraging point in the journey, Uncle Jeff appeared as promised, having ridden horseback over the great Sierra Nevada to meet his long-expected relatives. After a joyful reunion in the midst of the wilderness, they navigated the difficult, steep trail through Carson Canyon together. Charles remembered his joy at leaving behind the arid plains with their caustic dust and relishing the cool meadows and pine-scented slopes of the Sierra Nevada. Snowbanks provided refreshment for the family, while they enjoyed the breath-taking views of today's Lake Tahoe and purple sunsets shining off California's snowcapped peaks. After the most rugged sections of trail were past, Uncle Jeff rode ahead to Sutter Creek to prepare for the family's arrival.

Limping along, the little family found the way excruciatingly slow. Interestingly, Charles reported being delayed on the trail by huge freight wagons carrying supplies and mining machinery from Sacramento to the many burgeoning mines on the west-facing slopes of the Sierras. The teamsters, hurrying to beat the impending autumn snowstorms, nevertheless halted to question the family about their dilapidated, worn-out appearance, their wagon skeleton, and their long overland journey. Pulling off the road frequently to allow the freight teams to pass, sometimes twenty or thirty at a time, the Trues made little progress as they watched the snow creep down the mountains.

Charles reported seeing the evidence of much mining activity as they wound along the trail: prospect holes, mounds of rocks and dirt, sluice boxes, and especially Chinese miners reworking the tailings. Passing through several mining towns, he saw thousands of excavations, young miners working their claims, primitive shanties, and even a daily stagecoach headed for Missouri. As they passed through each camp, they brought much attention to themselves by their bedraggled appearance and their exhausted animals, which would lie down in their tracks at every opportunity.

Finally they reached Sutter Creek, their final destination. Charles was glad they arrived in the dark, so they could straggle into their new hometown unobserved. Gladly, they made their tired way to Jefferson Tarr's warm and welcoming hilltop ranch, where, in Charles's words, ". . . our journey across the Great American Desert to the Golden Shores of California came to an end."

FREIGHT WAGONS SIMILAR TO THOSE ENCOUNTERED BY CHARLES
FREDERICK TRUE AND HIS FAMILY IN THE SIERRA NEVADA MOUNTAINS.
WISCONSIN HISTORICAL SOCIETY, WHI-2807

The True family lived in Calaveras County, California, for many years. Charles worked and studied and eventually became a teacher and then principal of Wilson Elementary School in Alameda. He married and had three children, one of whom was born when he and his family moved to the Hawaiian Islands for a few years. He later returned to the California that he loved. There, true to his life-long habit, he spent long hours exploring the nearby mountain trails by himself, remembering his long-ago journey that brought him and his family safely to the land of "Golden Shores." Finally, when he was in his seventies, he recorded his memoirs, ensuring that the story of the True family's remarkable overland trek would be preserved forever.

TROUBLE IN DEATH VALLEY
The Story of John Wells Brier

When he wrote his memoirs half a century later, John Wells Brier vividly recalled the evening when he sat exhausted on Death Valley's parched desert sand. A boy of six traveling overland with his family, he had trudged all day across this stark land. Young John thought his small, energetic mother had never looked so weary, and he only hoped his father's fervent prayers for deliverance would be answered. He wished desperately for a drink for himself and his brothers, Christopher Columbus Brier (age eight) and Kirke White Brier (age four), but there was no water anywhere, and everyone was too worn-out to move another step.

The desert's arid desolation stretched as far he could see. John shut his eyes, trying not to think about how hungry he was. There was hardly a morsel of food left. It seemed as if there were nothing left on earth but this endless place—usually terribly hot, but today cold and windy—and no one knew the way out of this vast desert. John was too tired to think much about the starving oxen, but their pitiful lowing saddened him. He was glad they no longer had to pull the heavy covered wagon; the Briers had burned it for fuel and abandoned their belongings a few days earlier.

The trip hadn't always been this hard. John and his family had set out from Utah Lake, just south of the Great Salt Lake, on September 30, 1849. His father, James Welsh Brier, was a minister, and his mother, Juliette (or Julia), was a remarkably strong and determined parent to the couple's three boys. The family joined a party of about five hundred travelers with more than one hundred wagons hurrying to the goldfields of California. The group hired a guide, Captain Jefferson Hunt, who promised to deliver the emigrants to the Spanish settlement of Los Angeles in nine short weeks for only ten dollars a wagon. Spirits were high as the party set off with fresh teams of oxen and just enough provisions to make the trip. The lightly loaded wagons would allow the oxen to travel relatively quickly along the Old Spanish Trail.

Contrary to the travelers' wishes, though, the trip went slowly. The surrounding countryside grew drier than ever, and the emigrants worried that they would never reach California before their scanty provisions gave out. When seven of the nine weeks had gone by with only a third of the distance covered, the "spirit of discontent grew towards open revolt," wrote John Wells Brier in his memoirs. He remembered being afraid of the silent, serious guide whose errors, it was felt, had delayed the party to the point of danger.

Camping in today's southwestern Utah, they encountered another party also headed to California. The new travelers were guiding themselves with an unofficial map drawn by an old trapper showing an alternate route due west. The map showed the route to be far shorter and interspersed with tempting springs. Best of all, it promised to take the emigrants to Owen's Lake—which was well along the distance to the goldfields—within two weeks.

Immediately the men held a conference. Although Captain Hunt warned against the untraveled route, all but a handful of wagons joined the newcomers and veered off the Old Spanish Trail into

(LEFT TO RIGHT) JULIETTE BRIER, CHRISTOPHER COLUMBUS BRIER,
KIRKE WHITE BRIER, REVEREND JAMES BRIER, AND JOHN WELLS BRIER.
BEAR STATE LIBRARY

the arid wilderness to the west without a guide. The Briers were among them.

Within a few short days, the travelers encountered an impassable deep gorge that stretched before them. More than half of the group turned around to rejoin Captain Hunt. The others, including the Brier family, sent scouts ahead who returned with the news that there was a way around the chasm and a stopping place with abundant water, later known as Mountain Meadows. They pushed on and camped at this welcome site.

The winter weather was chilly, but the wagon travelers set out again, tiny specks winding through the huge valley at the base of the Timpanute Mountains, where John described the landscape and bunch grass as "exceedingly picturesque." After fifty miles, they descended into a wide desert with what appeared to be Owen's Lake in the distance. As the party hurried toward the nearest shore, the lake disappeared, and the travelers grimly realized the whole vision had been a mirage. Sorely disappointed, they stopped at a "basin of mud, with a shallow pool of brine" instead. With dust covering every inch of their bodies and belongings, and the need for drinking water growing with each mile, the mirage was a crushing disappointment.

John remembered little of that part of the journey except that the party began to split up, with every man for himself. He reported that small groups left them at several different places as the family struggled along, ever mindful of the area's harsh realities, the oxen's worsening condition, and the cumbersome wagons. Before long it was clear that they must abandon their wagons if they wanted to survive, an event that John recalled vividly. The day was cold and a sharp wind blew stinging sand against the walls of the family's camping tent. The Briers burned their wagon for fuel and left behind their treasured belongings. Then, loading their paltry supplies on their emaciated animals, they set out on foot with their few remaining companions, their rations nearly gone.

While Reverend Brier scouted ahead, the boys and their mother followed, herding the cattle. By then it was mid-December. After many days of "bitter travel," they reached the dry bed of the Amargosa River and camped near a muddy pool of water somewhere near the present-day border of Nevada and California. Filling their canteens, they moved on through the dry mountainous terrain. The next day they found themselves at the summit of a mountain pass "where there was no water, no grass, no fuel—nothing but a low, tubular plant . . . that rattled desolately in the north wind," John recalled. Spirits were low, but the Reverend Brier, with his deep faith and persevering nature, assured the party that God would not forsake them. Juliette Brier agreed and kept up a brave front for her three young sons. When her husband climbed a nearby mountain to see what lay ahead, he spotted a faraway oasis of water and grass—this time not a mirage—and knew their prayers had been answered.

The party headed slowly toward the clear springs. Expecting to reach the area in just a few hours, the men went ahead, with Juliette and the boys following as fast as they could. Little Kirke gave out, and Juliette carried him on her back until he could walk again. Although she was faint from exhaustion and thirst, she knew that to give up meant certain death. Sinking to her knees, she would rest a moment, then stagger on with her boys. Night fell. They followed the trail in the starlight until, six miles from the oasis, they caught up with the men. By then Kirke was moaning for a drink, almost unconscious from lack of water, and John and his older brother were near exhaustion. Reverend Brier took his youngest son on his back and hastened to the spring in order to save his life. The others followed, reaching the water in the early morning hours of Christmas Day 1849. They rested in the lush setting, enjoying the abundant water of "every degree of temperature." There they camped and killed an ox for dinner. Reverend Brier summoned the energy to give a humorous sermon to lift his boys' spirits and remind everyone of home.

The group's situation was so desperate that a wrong turn could bring death. Searching carefully, the party's scouts found the fresh wagon tracks of another party and decided it would be best to follow them. The tracks led straight into eastern California's Death Valley.

It didn't take long for the Briers to overtake the new travelers, who turned out to be forty-niners working their way to the California goldfields. These thirty or more men were known as the "Jayhawkers" and, along with the Briers, were among the first Caucasians to venture, if unwillingly, into Death Valley. They offered to let Juliette and James Brier stay behind with their children while they pushed on to civilization for help. But Juliette, unwilling to be abandoned, insisted on continuing the journey. Although the Jayhawkers were slightly reluctant to allow a woman and children to join their overland trek, they promised to help. The group struggled ahead, inch by inch, hour by hour, enduring the harsh environment and terrible thirst. Death Valley, it seemed, had been aptly named, and John remembered the miserable and uncertain crossing all his life.

Still ahead the arid Panamint Mountains and then the Panamint Desert stretched forth, a wilderness nearly impossible to cross in their condition. There was no water amid the odd vegetation and barren, unfriendly boulders, and, to make matters worse, the western wind blew sand from the bare dunes into their faces. The travelers, not knowing the best route, wound through the area, prolonging their ordeal with wrong turns and meandering attempts to reach safety. John tried to encourage his little brother by telling him of the water and food they would soon find, but the little boy wailed for a drink. The children's tongues were swollen, their lips cracked and bleeding. The cattle, too, were frenzied for lack of water. Reverend Brier climbed a distant rocky ridge, found a patch of snow, and returned carrying all he could in an old shirt.

Meanwhile the travelers were so weak that even performing necessary daily tasks became difficult. Reverend Brier himself began to fail and had to use two walking sticks to stumble ahead. Food was so scarce that one of the Jayhawkers, John recalled, chewed on a tallow candle to survive. Fortunately the Briers had coffee, which they relied upon to disguise the bad taste of the scant water available. Juliette later wrote, "Our coffee was a wonderful help and had that given out, I know we would have died."

When more mountains arose ahead of them, the party divided to cross by different routes. The route the Briers took was dangerous and steep, with only a trickle of water at the summit, but with sheer determination they crossed successfully and were reunited with the main body of the Jayhawkers on the other side. By then some of the travelers had died from exhaustion and the "whole party was in desperate emergency," John wrote, and his mother echoed in her later writings, "Every step I expected to sink down and die."

Once again scouts were sent out to find water. John remembered waiting for them to return to camp, but when all but one came back without locating a spring or even a muddy puddle, it looked as though death from thirst was inevitable. Juliette Brier refused to give up hope. Determined to get her family through the ordeal, she encouraged them repeatedly, certain that her prayers would be answered. Just as she was reassuring them, the last of the scouts hurried up with the news that he had, miraculously, found a plentiful water source. The Briers rejoiced and gave thanks to

God as the scout led his weary followers to the lifesaving spot that they called Providence Spring.

There they camped for two days, killing another ox for meat to replenish their strength. Even with rest and food, the emigrants were near death but, determined to reach the fertile valleys beyond the deserts, they pushed on, using every ounce of their strength to keep moving and to herd the remaining cattle with them. Bedraggled, dirty, and utterly worn-out, they were saved from death once again at the edge of the Mojave Desert by a pool of "turbid" water. John wrote that they "cared little for the deposit of yellow mud at the bottom of the coffee pot. . . ." Not far beyond, another of the travelers died.

At long last, and much to their joy, the desert land fell behind them, and they slowly emerged into an area of good grass for the cattle. It was there they discovered a stream leading westward that they followed, profoundly grateful for the green vegetation, wildlife, and trees that appeared—and for the deliverance from the harsh deserts. Eventually they entered a parklike area with large shade trees and, incredibly, a well-worn trail. Here the party camped for the night as a cool mist covered the green hills.

In the morning the campers heard the lowing of cattle, and thinking them to be strays, shot and killed one of them for food. Responding to the gunfire, a group of horsemen rode into the clearing, led by the Spanish owner of the cattle. Expecting the old rancher to be angry and demand restitution for the dead animal, the men of the Brier party prepared for the worst. But the gentleman proprietor of the sprawling ranch took one astounded look at the skeletal, emaciated group before him and immediately sprang into action. The destitute travelers were taken at once to his large, inviting hacienda. There, at the Rancho de San Francisquito owned by the Del Valle family, a feast was prepared. The señora of the ranch greeted Juliette Brier with tears of warmth and sympathy and offered every comfort to the starving travelers.

The grueling overland trip through Death Valley and its sur-roundings was over. It was February 4, 1850. John later wrote about his appreciation for the rich valleys and azure skies they had reached—and for the generous, cordial hospitality of the Spanish people they encountered. A doctor from the settlement at Los Angeles, who had heard from earlier emigrants about the plight of those crossing the deserts, came out to meet them and cared for them as they recovered from near starvation. After resting for a time with their kind hosts, the travelers moved on to the Mission of San Fernando, where they again were welcomed with warmth and a feast from the overflowing orchards of oranges, olives, and pomegranates. The newcomers were given horses to ride the last twenty miles to Los Angeles, the end of their journey. A comfort-able saddle was made for Mrs. Brier from two pillows, and little Kirke was tied onto the gentle pony's back behind her. The cross-ing to Los Angeles was "a pleasure trip," John remembered.

The doctor took the Briers to his home, where they were made comfortable and where they learned some necessary Spanish words from the doctor's wife. Reverend Brier sold the oxen his family had herded through the deserts, which were well trained and therefore in demand even though they were thin and tough. With the profit he was able to purchase half an interest in a hotel that also housed a blacksmith shop, a barber shop, and a bakery. There the family settled, serving boarders amid the quaint settlement of adobe houses and its busy marketplace. John and his brothers attended a nearby private school while Reverend Brier resumed his preaching and became a well-known Methodist missionary.

The Jayhawkers who survived the trip with the Briers scattered to the winds. But the bonds formed on that grueling and extraordinary journey were strong, and, throughout the years, the members of the Death Valley Party stayed in touch, reuniting occasionally and recalling their ordeal. At least one of those later reunions took place at the home of elderly Juliette Brier, who lived to the age of ninety-nine and is still remembered for her courage and heroism in the face of death and destitution. John Wells Brier, who recalled his childhood journey with such clarity, followed in his father's footsteps, choosing for his life's work to teach others about the God who delivered him and his family from the valley of the shadow of death. ▓

BIBLIOGRAPHY

General Sources:

Diaries, Memoirs, Letters and Reports Along the Trails West. www.over-land.com/
diaries.html. Last updated April 21, 2000. Accessed May 15, 2000.

Horn, Huston, and the editors of Time-Life Books. *The Pioneers.* Time-Life
Books–The Old West Books. New York: Time-Life Books, 1979.

Kimball, Violet T. *Stories of Young Pioneers in Their Own Words.* Missoula,
Montana: Mountain Press, 2000.

Lamar, Howard C. "Rites of Passage: Young Men and Their Families in the
Overland Trails Experience, 1843–64." In *'Soul Butter and Hog Wash' and
Other Essays on the American West,* edited by Thomas G. Alexander. Provo,
Utah: Brigham Young University Press, 1978.

Morgan, Dale, ed. *Overland in 1846: Diaries and Letters of the California-
Oregon Trail.* Volumes I and II. Lincoln and London: University of Nebraska
Press, 1993.

Palmer, Rosemary Gudmundson. *Voices from the Trail: Young Pioneers on the Platte River Road Between 1841 and 1869.* (Microfiche of a dissertation submitted to the Division of Lifelong Learning and Instruction and The Graduate School of the University of Wyoming in partial fulfillment of the requirements for the degree of Doctor of Philosophy in Education.) Laramie, Wyoming. August 1997. (UMI Microform #9805274. Copyright 1997 by UMI Company, 300 North Zeeb Road, Ann Arbor, MI 48103.)

Werner, Emmy E. *Pioneer Children on the Journey West.* Boulder, San Francisco, Oxford: Westview Press, 1995.

West, Elliot. *Growing Up with the Country: Childhood on the Far Western Frontier.* Albuquerque: University of New Mexico Press, 1989.

Jesse A. Applegate:

Applegate, Jesse. *A Day with the Cow Column.* Fairfield, Washington: Ye Galleon Press, 1990.

Coffman, Lloyd W. *Blazing a Wagon Trail to Oregon: A Weekly Chronicle of the Great Migration of 1843.* Enterprise, Oregon: Echo Books, 1993.

Ghent, W. J. *The Road to Oregon: A Chronicle of the Great Emigrant Trail.* New York: Tudor Publishing Co., 1934.

Rucker, Maude A. *The Oregon Trail and Some of Its Blazers.* New York: Walter Neal, 1930.

Welborn Beeson:

Ashland Tidings. Newspaper abstracts printed as microfilmed. Lida Childers and Ruby Lacy. Vol. 6: January 1892 to December 1893. Copyright 1990, pp. 112–15.

Beeson, Welborn. *The Oregon & Applegate Trail Diary of Welborn Beeson in 1853.* The unabridged diary with introduction and contemporary comments by Bert Webber, 1987. Published by Webb Research Group (no city or date given). Distributed by Pacific Northwest Books Company (Pioneer Trails Books Company), Medford, Oregon.

Jones, Anne. "John Beeson Human Rights Activist." www.so-oregon.com/color/beeson/beeson.html. Accessed March 27, 2001.

Beeson Papers. A Beeson family tree, a description of the Brophy-Beeson papers held at the Huntington Library in California, a synopsis of Welborn Beeson's life written by volunteer Edward B. Jorgenson of the Southern Oregon Historical Society, descriptions of Beeson photos available.

John Wells Brier:

Brier, John Wells. "Death Valley Party of 1849." *Out West Magazine.* March 1903, pp. 326–35, April 1903, pp. 456–65.

Brier, Juliette. "Our Christmas Amid the Terrors of Death Valley 1849." *San Francisco Call,* vol. LXXXV, no. 25, December 25, 1898, p. 19.

"Map of the Old Spanish Trail, 1846." www/homesteadmuseum.org/family/mapost.htm. Accessed February 11, 2001.

Wheat, Carl I. "The Forty-niners in Death Valley: A Tentative Census." www.scvhistory.com/scvhistory/wheat-49ers.htm. Accessed January 26, 2001. Originally published in *The Quarterly* of the Historical Society of Southern California, December 1939.

Wheat, Carl I. "Trailing the Forty-niners Through Death Valley." *Sierra Club Bulletin,* June 1939, pp. 74–108.

Elisha Brooks:

Brooks, Elisha. *A Pioneer Mother of California.* San Francisco: Harr Wagner Publishing Co., 1922.

Kimball, Violet T. *Stories of Young Pioneers in Their Own Words.* Missoula, Montana: Mountain Press, 2000.

Moynihan, Ruth Barnes. "Children and Young People on the Overland Trail." *Western Historical Quarterly,* July 1975, pp. 279–94.

Stewart, George R. *The California Trail: An Epic with Many Heroes.* New York: McGraw-Hill Book Company, Inc., 1962.

Henry and John Ferguson:

Bruff, J. Goldsborough. *Gold Rush: The Journals, Drawings, and Other Papers of J. Goldsborough Bruff.* New York: Columbia University Press, 1949.

Ferguson, Henry O. "The Moving of W. W. Ferguson and Family from Owen County, Indiana, to Iowa Territory in 1844." Typed transcript from the University of California's Bancroft Library.

Ferguson, Henry O. (assisted in memory by J. N. Ferguson). "Journey to California, 1849." January 16, 1918, Healdsburg, California. Typed transcript from the University of California's Bancroft Library.

Wexler, Sanford. *Westward Expansion: An Eyewitness History.* New York and Oxford: Facts on File, 1991.

Octavius M. Pringle:

Pringle, O. M. *Magic River Deschutes and Experience of an Emigrant Boy in 1846.* Fairfield, Washington: Ye Galleon Press, 1970.

Pringle, Virgil Kellog. *Overland Diary, 1846, and Daily Diary, 1853–56.* Copy of the original in the Pacific University Archives, Harvey W. Scott Memorial Library, Forest Grove, Oregon.

O'Brien, Mary Barmeyer. "Grandmother on Horseback: The Story of Tabitha Moffatt Brown." In *Heart of the Trail: The Stories of Eight Wagon Train Women.* Helena, Montana: Falcon Publishing Co., Inc., 1997.

Brigham H. Roberts:

Church Education System (prepared by). *Church History in the Fullness of Times: The History of the Church of Jesus Christ of Latter-day Saints.* Salt Lake City: The Church of Jesus Christ of Latter-day Saints, 1992.

Madsen, Truman G. *Defender of the Faith: The B. H. Roberts Story.* Salt Lake City: Bookcraft, Inc., 1980.

Roberts, B. H. *The Autobiography of B. H. Roberts.* Edited by Gary James Bergera. Salt Lake City: Signature Books, 1990.

Moses Schallenberger:

Graydon, Charles K. "Trail of the First Wagons over the High Sierra." *Overland Journal, The Quarterly Journal of the Oregon-California Trails Association*, vol. 4, no.1, Winter 1986, pp. 4–17.

Gudde, Erwin G., ed. "Robinson Crusoe in the Sierra Nevada: The Story of Moses Schallenberger at Donner Lake in 1844–45." *Sierra Club Bulletin*, vol. 36, no. 5, May 1951, pp. 19–29.

Stewart, George R. *The Opening of the California Trail*. The Story of the Stevens Party from the reminiscences of Moses Schallenberger as set down for H. H. Bancroft about 1885, edited and expanded by Horace S. Foote in 1888, and now edited with introduction, notes, maps, and illustrations by George R. Stewart. Berkeley and Los Angeles: University of California Press, 1953.

———. *The California Trail: An Epic with Many Heroes*. New York: McGraw-Hill Book Company, Inc., 1962.

"The Schallenberger–Breen Cabin." Text of a plaque located near the site of the Schallenberger–Breen Cabin. Erected by the Nevada County Historical Landmarks Commission and the California Department of Parks and Recreation, August 19, 1995. www.jdds.com/donner/schall.htm. Accessed July 22, 2001.

Charles Frederick True:

Editors of Time-Life Books. *The American Story: Settling the West*. Alexandria, Virginia: Time-Life Books, 1996.

Gunn, LaDonna. "First Gold Rushers to Pike's Peak (1858–1859)." Old Colorado City Historical Society. history.oldcolo.com/history/genhist/mining/goldrush.html. Accessed November 12, 2001.

True, Charles Frederick. *The Overland Memoir of Charles Frederick True: A Teenager on the California Trail, 1859*. Edited by Sally Ralston True, Ph.D. Independence, Missouri: Oregon-California Trails Association, 1993.

Werner, Emmy E. *Pioneer Children on the Journey West*. Boulder, San Francisco, Oxford: Westview Press, 1995.

INDEX

A

Alameda, 83
Alexander Valley, 30
Alford family, 27–28
Applegate, Charles, 2
Applegate, Cynthia, 9
Applegate, Edward, 8
Applegate, Elisha, 8
Applegate, Jesse A., 1–12
Applegate, Lindsay, 2
Applegate, Mack, 3, 8
Applegate Trail, 10, 34, 39, 45–46
Applegate, Warren, 8–9

B

Beeson, Ann, 42–47
Beeson, John, 42–47
Beeson, Welborn, 41–49
Ben Lomond, California, 59
Big Sandy River, 15, 27, 67
Blackfeet Indians, 57
Blue Mountains, 6
Bountiful, 68

Brier, Christopher
    Columbus, 85–93
Brier, James Welsh, 86–93
Brier, John Wells, 85–94
Brier, Juliette, 86–94
Brier, Kirk White, 85–93
Brooks, Elijah, 52
Brooks, Elisha, 51–59
Brooks, Eliza, 51–58
Brophy, Mary Catherine, 47
Brown, Tabitha, 32
Bruff, Joseph
    Goldsborough, 28
Bruff's Camp, 28

C

Calapooia Mountains, 37
Calaveras County, California, 83
California, 24
California gold camps, 27–28
California settlements, 13
California Trail, 33, 45, 57, 78
Carson Canyon, 80
Carson, Kit, 46

Carson River, 80
Cascades, The, 9
Caw Indians, 3
Cayuse Indians, 6
Chicago, 63
Chimney Rock, 33, 67
Chinese miners, 81
Chipman, William
  Henry, 61, 66
cholera, 26–27, 53
Church of Latter-day
  Saints, 70
Columbia River, 1, 7, 9, 12
Continental Divide, 5, 14, 44
Council Bluffs, 14, 52, 63
Crow Indians, 55

D

Dallas, Oregon, 10
Dalles, The, 9
Day with the Cow Column, A, 2
Death Valley, 85, 90
Death Valley Party, 94
Del Valle family, 93
Deschutes River, 39
Devil's Gate, 67, 78
Donner Lake, 15
Donner Party, 15

E

Echo Canyon, 68
Everitt, Fanny, 22

F

Feather River, 27, 58
Ferguson, Amanda, 24
Ferguson,
  Elizabeth, 24, 28, 30
Ferguson, Henry, 23–30
Ferguson, John, 23–30
Ferguson, Martha, 24
Ferguson, Mary
  (mother), 23, 30
Ferguson, Mary (daughter), 30
Ferguson, Nancy, 24
Ferguson, Paris, 24
Ferguson, W. W., 23
Ferguson, William, 30
Fort Boise, 6
Fort Bridger, 5, 68
Fort Hall, 5, 15, 33, 78
Fort Laramie, 5, 14, 26, 32, 43,
  75, 77
Fort Vancouver, 9
Fort Walla Walla, 7, 10
Foster, Joseph, 18
Four Mile Desert, 79
Frémont, John, 5, 42

G

gold rush, 24
Goose Lake, 27, 46
Grand Ronde Valley, 6
Great Emigration, 2
Great Migration of 1843, 2
Great Salt Lake, 62, 86
Green River, 5, 14, 27, 45, 78

H

Hudson's Bay Company, 7, 9
Humboldt River, 15, 27, 45, 57,
    78, 79
Humboldt wolves, 79
Hunt, Captain Jefferson, 86

I

Idaho, 5
Independence, Missouri, 2
Independence Rock, 14, 26,
    55, 67
Iowa, 23

J

Jayhawkers, 90–91, 94
John Bright, 63

K

Kansas River, 3
Kirkpatrick, Reverend J. S., 24
Klamath Lake, 46

L

Lake Tahoe, 81
Lander Road, 78
Laramie Peak, 43
Laramie Plains, 54
Lassen Meadows, 45
Lassen Trail, 27
Little Blue River, 3
Liverpool, 63
Los Angeles, 86, 93

M

Martin, Dennis, 21
Marysville, California, 30
McClellan, Alexander, 2
McLoughlin, Dr. John, 9
Mission of San Fernando, 93
Mississippi River, 41–42, 52
Missouri, 13
Missouri River, 14, 43, 52,
    63, 74
Mojave Desert, 92
Monterey, 22

Montgomery, Allen, 18

Mormon faith, 62

Mormon Trail, 72

Mount Hood, 7

Mountain Meadows, 88

Murphy, John, 14

N

Narrative Across the Rocky Mountains, 42

Nebraska Territory, 74

Nevada, 15, 45

New York, 63

Niagara Falls, 63

North Platte River, 76

O

Old Spanish Trail, 86

Omaha, Nebraska, 24, 74

Oregon, 2, 6, 9, 10

Oregon Militia, 47

Oregon Territory, 5

Oregon Trail, 12, 78

Osage River, 1

Overland Memoir of Charles Fredrick True: A Teenager on the California Trail, 1859, The, 74

Owatonna, Minnesota, 74

Owen's Lake, 86, 88

P

Panamint Desert, 90

Panamint Mountains, 90

Pawnee Indians, 24, 26, 51, 53, 77

Perpetual Emigration Fund, 63

Pike's Peak, 74

Pitt River, 27

Plains Indian territory, 3

Platte River, 3–4, 24, 26, 43, 53, 61, 64, 67, 73–75

Portland, Oregon, 39

prairie dogs, 4

Prineville, 39

Pringle, Clark, 37

Pringle Falls, 39

Pringle, Octavius M., 31–39

Pringle, Pherne, 32, 37

Pringle, Virgil, 32–34

Providence Spring, 92

R

Rancho de San Francisquito, 92

Recollections of My Boyhood, 2

Roberts, Ann, 62

Roberts, Annie, 68

Roberts, Benjamin, 62

Roberts, Brigham
Henry, 61–72

Roberts, Mary, 62–70

Roberts, Thomas, 67

Rockies, 78

Rogue River Valley, 43, 47

S

Sacramento, 81

Sacramento River
Valley, 27, 57

Salem, Oregon, 10, 37, 39

Salt Creek Valley, 10

Salt Lake City, 63, 67

Salt Lake Valley, 68

San Francisco, 58

San Jose, 22

Scott's Bluff, 33

Shallenberger, Maggie, 22

Shallenberger, Moses, 13–22

Shoshone Indians, 5, 57

Sierra Nevada Mountains, 13, 15,
27, 30, 57, 79, 80

Sioux Indians, 33, 54, 77, 78

Skunk River, 41

Smith, Thomas L.
"Peg-leg," 15

Snake Indians, 5, 44

Snake River, 5, 78

Soda Springs, Idaho, 5, 45

South Pass, 5, 14, 44, 78

South Platte River, 4

Steamboat Springs, 5

Stevens, Captain Elisha, 20

Stevens-Townsend-Murphy
Party, 14, 15

Sublette Cutoff, 78

Sutter Creek, 81

Sutter's Fort, 22

Sweetwater River, 4, 14,
43, 55, 67, 78

T

Talent, Oregon, 47

Tarr, Jefferson, 79

Timpanute Mountains, 88

Townsend, Dr. John, 13, 15

Townsend, Mrs. John, 13

Truckee, 15

Truckee River, 15, 58

True, Carro, 73, 75

True, Charles Fredrick, 73–83

True, Elizabeth, 74

True, Ira, 74

U

Umatilla River, 6

Umpqua River Valley, 10

University of Deseret, 70

University of Utah, 70

Utah, 86

Utah Lake, 86

Utah Territory, 62–63

W

Walla Walla, 2

Watson, Virginia, 10

Whitman, Dr. Marcus, 2, 5, 6

Whitman Mission, 6

Whitman, Narcissa, 6

Willamette River, 7, 9

Willamette Valley, 9, 33, 37

Wilson Elementary School, 83

Wind River Range, 33

World War I, 70

Wyoming, 4, 5

Y

Yuba County, 30

Yuba River, 18, 21

Z

Zion, 72

ABOUT THE AUTHOR

Mary Barmeyer O'Brien was born and raised in Missoula, Montana, and received a B.A. in Sociology from Linfield College in McMinnville, Oregon. She is the author of two previous books about pioneers on the overland trails, *Toward the Setting Sun: Pioneer Girls Traveling the Overland Trails* and *Heart of the Trail: The Stories of Eight Wagon Train Women.* She has also written a biography for young readers called *Jeannette Rankin: Bright Star in the Big Sky,* and her magazine articles for both children and adults have appeared in many national magazines. Mary works from her home in Polson, Montana. She and her husband, Dan, a high school science teacher, have two daughters and a son.